Bloom's BioCritiques:

Joseph Conrad

Bloom's BioCritiques

Dante Alighieri
Maya Angelou
Jane Austen
The Brontë Sisters
Lord Byron
Geoffrey Chaucer
Anton Chekhov
Joseph Conrad
Stephen Crane
Charles Dickens
Emily Dickinson
William Faulkner
F. Scott Fitzgerald
Robert Frost
Ernest Hemingway
Langston Hughes
Stephen King
Arthur Miller
John Milton
Toni Morrison
Edgar Allan Poe
J. D. Salinger
William Shakespeare
John Steinbeck
Henry David Thoreau
Mark Twain
Alice Walker
Walt Whitman
Tennessee Williams

Bloom's BioCritiques

JOSEPH CONRAD

Edited and with an introduction by
Harold Bloom
Sterling Professor of the Humanities
Yale University

CHELSEA HOUSE
PUBLISHERS
A Haights Cross Communications Company
Philadelphia

Library of Congress Cataloging-in-Publication Data.

Joseph Conrad / edited and with an introduction by Harold Bloom.
         p. cm. -- (Bloom's biocritiques)
Includes bibliographical references and index.
    ISBN 0-7910-6371-2
  1. Conrad, Joseph, 1857–1924--Criticism and interpretation. I.
Bloom, Harold. II. Series.
    PR6005.04 Z74964 2003
    823' .912--dc21

                                        2002154038

Chelsea House Publishers
1974 Sproul Road, Suite 400
Broomall, PA 19008-0914

http://www.chelseahouse.com

Contributing editor: Richard Ruppel

Cover design by Keith Trego

Cover: © Hulton-Deutsch Collections/CORBIS

Layout by EJB Publishing Services

CONTENTS

USER'S GUIDE

These volumes are designed to introduce the reader to the life and work of the world's literary masters. Each volume begins with Harold Bloom's essay "The Work in the Writer" and a volume-specific introduction also written by Professor Bloom. Following these unique introductions is an engaging biography that discusses the major life events and important literary accomplishments of the author under consideration.

Furthermore, each volume includes an original critique that not only traces the themes, symbols, and ideas apparent in the author's works, but strives to put those works into a cultural and historical perspective. In addition to the original critique is a brief selection of significant critical essays previously published on the author and his or her works followed by a concise and informative chronology of the writer's life. Finally, each volume concludes with a bibliography of the writer's works, a list of additional readings, and an index of important themes and ideas.

HAROLD BLOOM

The Work in the Writer

Literary biography found its masterpiece in James Boswell's *Life of Samuel Johnson*. Boswell, when he treated Johnson's writings, implicitly commented upon Johnson as found in his work, even as in the great critic's life. Modern instances of literary biography, such as Richard Ellmann's lives of W. B. Yeats, James Joyce, and Oscar Wilde, essentially follow in Boswell's pattern.

That the writer somehow is in the work, we need not doubt, though with William Shakespeare, writer-of-writers, we almost always need to rely upon pure surmise. The exquisite rancidities of the Problem Plays or Dark Comedies seem to express an extraordinary estrangement of Shakespeare from himself. When we read or attend *Troilus and Cressida* and *Measure for Measure*, we may be startled by particular speeches of Ulysses in the first play, or of Vincentio in the second. These speeches, of Ulysses upon hierarchy or upon time, or of Duke Vincentio upon death, are too strong either for their contexts or for the characters of their speakers. The same phenomenon occurs with Parolles, the military impostor of *All's Well That Ends Well*. Utterly disgraced, he nevertheless affirms: "Simply the thing I am/Shall make me live."

In Shakespeare, more even than in his peers, Dante and Cervantes, meaning always starts itself again through excess or overflow. The strongest of Shakespeare's creatures—Falstaff, Hamlet, Iago, Lear, Cleopatra—have an exuberance that is fiercer than their plays can contain. If Ben Jonson was at all correct in his complaint that "Shakespeare wanted art," it could have been only in a sense that he may not have intended. Where do the personalities of Falstaff or Hamlet touch a limit? What was it in Shakespeare that made the two parts of *Henry IV* and *Hamlet* into "plays unlimited"? Neither Falstaff nor Hamlet will be stopped: their wit, their beautiful, laughing speech, their intensity of being—all these are virtually infinite.

In what ways do Falstaff and Hamlet manifest the writer in the work? Evidently, we can never know, or know enough to answer with any authority. But what would happen if we reversed the question, and asked: How did the work form the writer, Shakespeare?

Of Shakespeare's inwardness, his biography tells us nothing. And yet, to an astonishing extent, Shakespeare created our inwardness. At the least, we can speculate that Shakespeare so lived his life as to conceal the depths of his nature, particularly as he rather prematurely aged. We do not have Shakespeare on Shakespeare, as any good reader of the Sonnets comes to realize: they do not constitute a key that unlocks his heart. No sequence of sonnets could be less confessional or more powerfully detached from the poet's self.

The German poet and universal genius, Goethe, affords a superb contrast to Shakespeare. Of Goethe's life, we know more than everything; I wonder sometimes if we know as much about Napoleon or Freud or any other human being who ever has lived, as we know about Goethe. Everywhere, we can find Goethe in his work, so much so that Goethe seems to crowd the writing out, just as Byron and Oscar Wilde seem to usurp their own literary accomplishments. Goethe, cunning beyond measure, nevertheless invested a rival exuberance in his greatest works that could match his personal charisma. The sublime outrageousness of the Second Part of *Faust*, or of the greater lyric and meditative poems, form a Counter-Sublime to Goethe's own daemonic intensity.

Goethe was fascinated by the daemonic in himself; we can doubt that Shakespeare had any such interests. Evidently, Shakespeare abandoned his acting career just before he composed *Measure for Measure* and *Othello*. I surmise that the egregious interventions by Vincentio and Iago displace the actor's energies into a new kind of mischief-making, a fresh opening to a subtler playwriting-within-the-play.

But what had opened Shakespeare to this new awareness? The answer is the work in the writer, *Hamlet* in Shakespeare. One can go further: it was not so much the play, *Hamlet*, as the character Hamlet, who changed Shakespeare's art forever.

Hamlet's personality is so large and varied that it rivals Goethe's own. Ironically Goethe's Faust, his Hamlet, has no personality at all, and is as colorless as Shakespeare himself seems to have chosen to be. Yet nothing could be more colorful than the Second Part of *Faust*, which is peopled by an astonishing array of monsters, grotesque devils, and classical ghosts.

A contrast between Shakespeare and Goethe demonstrates that in each—but in very different ways—we can better find the work in the person, than we can discover that banal entity, the person in the work. Goethe to many of his contemporaries, seemed to be a mortal god. Shakespeare, so far as we know, seemed an affable, rather ordinary fellow, who aged early and became somewhat withdrawn. Yet Faust, though Mephistopheles battles for his soul, is hardly worth the trouble unless you take him as an idea and not as a person. Hamlet is nearly every-idea-in-one, but he is precisely a personality and a person.

Would Hamlet be so astonishingly persuasive if his father's ghost did not haunt him? Falstaff is more alive than Prince Hal, who says that the devil haunts him in the shape of an old fat man. Three years before composing the final *Hamlet*, Shakespeare invented Falstaff, who then never ceased to haunt his creator. Falstaff and Hamlet may be said to best represent the work in the writer, because their influence upon Shakespeare was prodigious. W.H. Auden accurately observed that Falstaff possesses infinite energy: never tired, never bored, and absolutely both witty and happy until Hal's rejection destroys him. Hamlet too has infinite energy, but in him it is more curse than blessing.

Falstaff and Hamlet can be said to occupy the roles in Shakespeare's invented world that Sancho Panza and Don Quixote possess in Cervantes's. Shakespeare's plays from 1610 on (starting with *Twelfth Night*) are thus analogous to the Second Part of Cervantes's epic novel. Sancho and the Don overtly jostle Cervantes for authorship in the Second Part, even as Cervantes battles against the impostor who has pirated a continuation of his work. As a dramatist, Shakespeare manifests the work in the writer more indirectly. Falstaff's prose genius is revived in the scapegoating of Malvolio by Maria and Sir Toby Belch, while Falstaff's darker insights are developed by Feste's melancholic wit. Hamlet's intellectual resourcefulness, already deadly, becomes poisonous in Iago and in Edmund. Yet we have not crossed into the deeper abysses of the work in the writer in later Shakespeare.

No fictive character, before or since, is Falstaff's equal in self-trust. Sir John, whose delight in himself is contagious, has total confidence both in his self-awareness and in the resources of his language. Hamlet, whose self is as strong, and whose language is as copious, nevertheless distrusts both the self and language. Later Shakespeare is, as it were, much under the influence both of Falstaff and of Hamlet, but they tug him in opposite directions. Shakespeare's own copiousness of language is well-nigh incredible: a vocabulary in excess of twenty-one thousand words, almost eighteen hundred of which he coined himself. And of his word-hoard, nearly half are used only once each, as though the perfect setting for each had been found, and need not be repeated. Love for language and faith in language are Falstaffian attributes. Hamlet will darken both that love and that faith in Shakespeare, and perhaps the Sonnets can best be read as Falstaff and Hamlet counterpointing against one another.

Can we surmise how aware Shakespeare was of Falstaff and Hamlet, once they had played themselves into existence? *Henry IV, Part I* appeared in six quarto editions during Shakespeare's lifetime; *Hamlet* possibly had four. Falstaff and Hamlet were played again and again at the Globe, but Shakespeare knew also that they were being read, and he must have had contact with some of those readers. What would it have been like to discuss Falstaff or Hamlet with one of their early readers (presumably also part of their audience at the Globe), if you were the creator of such demiurges? The question would seem nonsensical to most Shakespeare scholars, but then these days they tend to be either ideologues or moldy figs. How can we recover the uncanniness of Falstaff and of Hamlet, when they now have become so familiar?

A writer's influence upon himself is an unexplored problem in criticism, but such an influence is never free from anxieties. The biocritical problem (which this series attempts to explore) can be divided into two areas, difficult to disengage fully. Accomplished works affect the author's life, and also affect her subsequent writings. It is simpler for me to surmise the effect of *Mrs. Dalloway* and *To the Lighthouse* upon Woolf's late *Between the Acts*, than it is to relate Clarissa Dalloway's suicide and Lily Briscoe's capable endurance in art to the tragic death and complex life of Virginia Woolf.

There are writers whose lives were so vivid that they seem sometimes to obscure the literary achievement: Byron, Wilde, Malraux, Hemingway. But most major Western writers do not live that exuberantly, and the greatest of all, Shakespeare, sometimes appears to have adopted the personal mask of colorlessness. And yet there are heroes of literature who struggled titanically with their own eras—Tolstoy, Milton, Victor Hugo—who nevertheless matter more for their works than their lives.

There are great figures—Emily Dickinson, Wallace Stevens, Willa Cather—who seem to have had so little of the full intensity of life when compared to the vitality of their work, that we might almost speak of the work in the work, rather than even of the work in a person. Emily Brontë might well be the extreme instance of such a visionary, surpassing William Blake in that one regard.

I conclude this general introduction to a series of literary bio-critiques by stating a tentative formula or principle for gauging the many ways in which the work influences the person and her subsequent, later work. Our influence upon ourselves is always related to the Shakespearean invention of self-overhearing, which I have written about in several other contexts. Life, as well as poetry and prose, is overheard rather than simply heard. The writer listens to herself as though she were somebody else, and the will to change begins to operate. The forces that live in us include the prior work we have done, and the dreams and waking visions that evade our dismissals.

HAROLD BLOOM

Introduction

Joseph Conrad's early life was outrageous enough even for a young Polish person-of-letters, let alone for an English writer. At twenty-seven he helped run a munitions operation for the Carlist rebels in Spain. Before it was over, he came close to being killed, attempted suicide, fell in love with a fatal beauty, and gambled on a grand scale. By four years later, he had begun a more conventional career in the British merchant marine, which continued until 1894, during which time he commanded his own vessel. For his remaining thirty years, he was a superb and successful novelist, bringing forth such masterworks as *Lord Jim*, *Nostromo*, *The Secret Agent*, *Under Western Eyes*, and *Victory*.

Conrad's *The Mirror of the Sea* and *A Personal Record* give us his own vision of his years as a sailor. Though books of considerable use and value, they do not aid me much in understanding the moral complexities of the great Conradian novels, *Nostromo* and *Victory* in particular. A great and complex artist, Conrad seems to me more influenced by a magnificent imagining like *Nostromo*, than by the events of his own life.

And yet where are the limits of Conrad's irony in *Nostromo*? The magnificent Nostromo is in love with his own magnificence, and though he is a hero of the people, he essentially is hollow. With few exceptions, all of Conrad's protagonists are hollow men. One of the many paradoxes of Conrad is that the mirror of the sea allows us to perceive an heroic ideal, one that is not available in Conrad's great fictions.

What are the limits of irony in Conrad? For Martin Price, a profoundly Conradian ironist, there are no limits. Price sees both the skepticism and the irony of *Lord Jim*, and yet also perceives its unrelenting Romanticism. Both are allowed their full eloquence, and neither can balance or negate the other. Price ranks *Nostromo* lower, because he sees the irony as triumphant there. Conrad, an astonishing artist, allows the reader to decide. As I age, I abandon my ironies and join Nostromo in his Garibaldi-like Romanticism. In Nostromo, it is flawed and corrupt, but what matter? What matters in Conrad is not *whether* you betray yourself: of course you must and will. Either you betray others, or yourself. Those are the Conradian options. Of course, others betray you, but that is of minor interest, another mere irony. Nostromo sells himself for silver, and yet betrays nothing except his own authentic splendor.

In Conrad, you submit to the destructive element, the sea of death: no character in all of Conrad has a Hamlet-like power of mind, unless it be Kurtz, in *Heart of Darkness*, and he is self-obliterated, pragmatically speaking. Edward Said shrewdly noted Conrad's persuasive insistence that we can survive, as persons and as writers, only through the agency of our eccentricities. What matters most in Conrad's view of the human is that each of us is unpredictable.

Is there a more profound reply to all historicizing and psychologizing over-interpretations than the unpredictability of the influence of a writer's own works upon her or his life? *Victory*, a novel I never weary of rereading, was superbly interpreted by the late R. W. B. Lewis as a grand exploitation of "the peculiar resources of the novel." It has been suggested, by several critics, that *Victory* (1934) is haunted by *King Lear*, since it echoes Lear's "Nothing will come of nothing." The effect of Conrad's major novels upon their creator was to confirm his nihilism, despite his courageous efforts to endow certain of his protagonists with a fundamental, decent integrity. The suicide of Decond in *Nostromo* seems to me the ultimate triumph of Conradian nihilism.

The major modern American novelists—Hemingway, Fitzgerald, above all Faulkner—were the heirs of Conrad's vision of the nihilistic center of all human experience. Conrad, a majestic personality, held his own against the darker aspects of life, but his own art mutated him into a Shakespearean nihilist.

AMY SICKELS

Biography of Joseph Conrad

LIVING APART

On the second day of Joseph Conrad's disastrous journey to the Congo, he wrote in his diary, "Feel considerably in doubt about the future. Think just now that my life amongst the people (white) around here cannot be very comfortable. Intend [to] avoid acquaintances as much as possible."(Meyers, 102) Conrad's trip to Africa would later inspire one of his best known works, *Heart Of Darkness*. Physically, the trip made him severely ill. Psychologically, the journey exacted a heavy toll on him, challenging his thoughts about human nature and exacerbating his own sense of isolation—an isolation which had started long ago. Conrad often felt as if he were living on the outside, from his early childhood years when his family was sentenced to live in exile in Russia, to the many years he spent in England, learning the language and becoming one of the century's most-respected writers.

Long before Conrad was born, Poland had lost its independence and was divided among Russia, Prussia, and Austria. Conrad's father, a Polish patriot, devoted his life to the cause of Polish independence, and his political activism led to his arrest and the deportation of his family. Young Conrad grew up as a Pole in the bitter, freezing environment of northern Russia. Having left Poland at the age of five, Conrad had no semblance of his father's devotion to this country.

Both his parents died by the time he was eleven, resulting in an even greater sense of loneliness for Conrad. Although he was taken under the good care of his relatives in Poland, he did not have a real home and moved often, fostering in him a sense of restlessness. These impressionable early years of his life were defined by loss and displacement, themes that would appear in much of his work.

While his father had been a Polish revolutionary, Conrad only wanted to escape this country that had given him nothing but heartache. Restless and eager for some place new, he left Poland to become a sailor, first in France, then England. When friends met Conrad for the first time, they were struck by his heavy Polish accent and foreign appearance—he did not "look" like an Englishman. Although he gained English citizenship, shortened his Polish name to the more English sounding, "Joseph Conrad," and lived most of his adult life in England, he never felt as if it were "home"—English humor often baffled him, and he did not feel connected to its customs or traditions.

Although he had made his residence in England, he continued to keep in touch with his family in Poland, and made several trips to the country he was so eager to leave. He stayed abreast of political concerns in Poland, and still felt connected, although tenuously, to his heritage and birth place.

When Conrad first began to write, he chose to write in English, his *third* acquired language, yet he did not even begin to teach himself English until he moved to England in his early twenties. Scholars often point out how remarkable it is to write such ambitious, poetic novels in a third-learned language. However, Conrad's decision to write in English and not Polish further divided him from his home-country.

In 1899, an attack on his character was made by another Polish writer. The philosopher Wincenty Lutoslawski claimed in the *Kraj*, a Polish journal published in St. Petersburg, that Conrad was justified in writing in English because he was not talented enough to write in Polish. He also declared that Conrad wrote in English to make more money. This article spawned a letter of response from the Polish novelist Eliza Orzeszkowa, who equated Conrad's emigration with betrayal:

> ... I must say that the gentleman who in English is writing novels which are widely read and bring good profit almost caused me a nervous attack ... Creative ability is the very crown of the plant, the very top of the tower, the very heart of the heart of the nation. And to take away from one's nation

this flower, this top, this heart and give it to the Anglo-Saxons who are not even lacking in bird's milk, for the only reason that they pay better for it—one cannot even think of it without shame. (Meyers, 189)

Conrad, who was struggling to pay his rent and accumulating debt, certainly wasn't profiting from the English language at the time, and he felt angered and wounded by these accusations.

Leaving Poland and renouncing his citizenship had always been a delicate topic with Conrad. His father had wanted to make him into a Polish patriot, but Conrad had not followed in his revolutionist footsteps; instead he left his country behind. He had adopted the English language, made English friends, and lived in England for most of his life. The criticism touched a raw nerve; Conrad was often plagued with guilt that he had betrayed his parent's alliances to Poland and their commitment to risking their lives for their country.

Interestingly, themes of betrayal appeared in his work, namely, *Lord Jim*, which he wrote after the attack by Orzeszkowa. This novel concerns a man who abandons his ship, based on a real incident Conrad had heard about.

The commentary by Orzeszkowa obviously bothered Conrad. He wrote to Jozef Korzeniowski (of no blood relation), librarian of the Polish Jagiellonian Library, in defense of himself: "And please let me add, dear Sir (for you may still be hearing this and that said of me) that I have in no way disavowed either my nationality or the name we share for sake of success." (Najder, 256) Conrad felt caught between his birth county and his adopted country, yet the divisions often overlapped, resembling his position in another significant division in his life—that of sailor and writer.

Conrad started sailing before he was twenty-years-old, and continued with this career for another twenty years. Furthermore, he didn't even start to write seriously until his early thirties. As a sailor, the rest of the crew often viewed him as an outsider, and Conrad felt more comfortable with literary people, not sailors. Yet, he was learning to be a writer even when he wasn't picking up a pen—by observing and gaining insight to people. Later, after he had given up sailing and writing had consumed him, the overlap between the two was obvious—he often wrote about his earlier sea-faring experiences, taking real events and turning them into fiction.

Most significantly, while he was in the Congo in 1890—originally hired to captain a ship—he was making the transition to a writing career. He felt like an outsider in the Congo—not just with the native Africans, but with his "own" people. On the outside, he witnessed the Europeans' barbarity and destruction, and for the first time, he began to keep a diary, writing down his observations. Before the trip to the Congo, Conrad had already started his first novel, and after the ill-fated trip, he would embark on one more journey. However, it was this crucial period in the Congo, where he was acutely aware of his isolation and position as an outsider that psychologically pushed Conrad from sailor to writer.

Although he experienced feelings of displacement all his life— from losing his parents to leaving his own country—these feelings also allowed him to observe those around him, an impetus for his writing. "We live, as we dream—alone," Conrad writes in *Heart of Darkness*. His isolation allowed him to step back from situations familiar to him, and write about them with a keen and unique perspective. His art could not exist without his pervasive feelings of living on the outside, and these feelings, in turn, were what led him to writing.

A LONELY CHILDHOOD

Joseph Conrad was born, Józef Teodor Konrad Walecz Korzeniowski, on December 3, 1857, one year after the Crimean War, in the vicinity of Berdichev of the Polish Ukraine, which was land then controlled by Russia. Poland had been invaded and partitioned over the years, and was divided up among Russia, Prussia, and Austria at the time of Conrad's birth. In the early 1800's, when Napoleon invaded Russia, the Poles hoped their country would be freed, however, the division remained. There were two failed Polish uprisings in 1830 and 1846, and Poland remained under the control of its neighboring countries.

Conrad's birthplace, the Polish Ukraine, was divided by four languages and four religions. Both of his parents belonged to the Polish land-owning nobility, the *szlachta*—a hereditary class below the aristocracy. Although the large group had modest incomes and occupations, they constituted the ruling class of Poland, and they were typically politically active, involved in such revolutions as the anti-Russian insurrections of 1794 and 1830.

Conrad's father Apollo Korzeniowski came from a family of patriots, whose estate had been confiscated by the Russian authorities after a national uprising. Apollo attended St. Petersburg University, studying literature, law, and languages, then left after six years without earning a degree. He had a passion for politics and writing, and he believed wholeheartedly that Poland would one day gain freedom and independence, sacrificing his life to this cause.

Conrad's mother, Ewelina Bobrowska (known as Ewa or Eva in English), was thirteen years younger than Apollo. Her family was less politically active than Apollo's, retaining their estates and staying more on the sidelines of political affairs. Eva grew up in a family with six brothers, and as the only daughter, the family felt very protective of her.

Apollo's political and artistic passions attracted Eva, and he felt drawn to her imaginative mind and kind personality. Although they had fallen in love, they did not marry for eight more years—Eva's father did not believe Apollo would make a suitable husband for his daughter. Apollo Korzeniowski, an idealist and political activist, owned no land and had no steady occupation, and he seemed irresponsible and rebellious.

However, five years after Eva's father's death, they were able to marry, now with the reluctant blessing of Eva's family. Marrying didn't change Apollo's personality. He failed to find steady work, and after squandering all of Eva's dowry, he focused all of his energy on writing and politics. He wrote a variety of plays, poems, and social satires, and committed himself to political activities. One year after Apollo and Eva married, they had their only child.

When Joseph Conrad turned three years old, his revolutionist father moved to Warsaw, ostensibly to direct a literary periodical. However, he soon became involved in underground political activities concerning Polish independence and nationalism. Several months later Eva and Joseph joined him in Warsaw; their flat, located on a main street in the city, became a meeting place for the underground political group City Committee.

One quiet night while Apollo was writing and Eva was reading, the doorbell rang. The Russian police quickly raided their flat and arrested Apollo, and he spent several months in prison. In his book, *Joseph Conrad: A Biography*, Jeffrey Meyers explains that one of Conrad's most telling memories from this time recalls when his mother dressed in all black to represent national mourning and took him to see his father. Conrad stood outside in the courtyard and saw his father staring at him through a barred window. (Meyers, 14) Political passions and revolutionary ideas were Conrad's earliest childhood memories; however, soon the boy's life would be consumed by turbulence and loss.

Letters Eva had written to Apollo were used as incriminating evidence in the trial, and both of Conrad's parents were convicted. The family was deported to Vologda in northern Russia, a city north of Moscow with freezing temperatures and a bleak environment. Under police escort, young Joseph also made the journey with his parents; he was five years old.

Both Joseph and his mother became sick on the arduous trip, suffering from cold and thirst, and Joseph nearly died. When they finally reached their destination, conditions did not improve. Their new life was filled with poverty, hardships, melancholy, and illness. They lived in a primitive log house, difficult to heat in the arctic temperatures. In a letter, Apollo described the severity of the environment:

> A year here has two seasons: white winter and green winter. The white winter lasts nine and a half months, the green winter two and a half. Now is the beginning of the green winter: it has been raining continually for twenty-one days and will do so till the end. During the white winter the temperature falls to minus twenty-five or thirty degrees and the wind blows from the White Sea....The air stinks of mud, birch tar and whale-oil: this is what we breathe. (Meyers, 16).

The brutal conditions of the climate coupled with the lack of health care led to Eva's struggle with tuberculosis. The authorities granted the family permission to relocate in Chernikov, a city with better weather and resources, but also with a political atmosphere quite hostile to Poles. Although his parents tried to shield him from this unfriendly climate, the mood of the place certainly shaped Conrad's childhood years, and solidified his anger and distrust toward Russians.

Not only was Conrad being raised in a place with harsh, crude conditions, but he was also growing up in an atmosphere of national defeat. The Polish insurrection of 1863, the event that his father had been helping to plan before he was arrested, had failed, and now Tsarist

Russia ruled much of Poland, forbidding even the teaching of the Polish language. The failed uprising led to terrible repercussions for the family—Apollo's father died on the way to join the Partisans, his older brother had been killed, and another brother was deported to Siberia. One of Eva's brothers was jailed and another died in a duel. Apollo, already inclined to pessimism, felt terribly defeated by the failed uprising.

Even though the physical conditions were better in Chernikov, Eva's health continued to worsen. Her health had always been weak, and these conditions debilitated her even more. One of her brothers, who had connections with the Russian Guards, arranged for her and Conrad to leave for three months and visit the family estate. Eva received medical attention, and Conrad, an only child who was used to being alone, had a chance to play with his cousins and escape the despair of his home. However, this freedom and happiness were short-lived. Although Eva continued to weaken, she and her son were forced to return to their home of exile. The disease lingered on, slowly killing her, and consuming the house with sadness and fear. In 1865, at thirty-two years old, Eva died.

At the time, Conrad was only seven-years-old. His sorrow and devastation at the death of his mother intensified his own health problems—lung infections, attacks of epilepsy, and later, migraines. Conrad was a pale, sickly, and delicate child. He grew up in a mournful, quiet home, pervasive with the atmosphere of death and loneliness, and the psychological mood affected his physical health. As an adult, he would be prone to illness, as well as being highly nervous and overly sensitive.

His father's pessimism and melancholy certainly influenced Conrad's own personality. Apollo, overcome with grief and guilt about his wife's death, admitted that his son's childhood was filled with sadness and isolation: "Poor child: he does not know what a contemporary playmate is." (Meyers, 23) He had no children to play with, no friends or siblings.

He spent his childhood at the side of his dying father, and off in corners reading—which offered an escape from the prevalent despair. A quiet child, he found hope in the worlds of his books and wildly active imagination, whereas reality only offered sadness and despair. At the age of five, Conrad had already become a voracious reader, devouring books in French and Polish. Later, in a letter to a friend an older Conrad wrote, "I don't know what would have become of me, if I had not been a reading boy." (Gillon, 5) He spent long hours alone, reading everything he could. He read a wide variety of books, including sea adventures, history, geography, and his father's translations of Hugo, Dickens, and Shakespeare. Although they lived a life of exile, books were usually available in the Korzeniowski home, and when they weren't, Conrad would read the same stories over and over again.

Even though his father was weak and melancholy, he continued to have a literary influence on his son, tutoring him in the importance of literature, and politics, hoping to instill in Conrad his own devotion and love for Poland. Despite everything that had happened, Apollo still believed in martyrdom for the sake of one's country, and felt that one must be a true Pole and resist Russian authority.

In a letter, Apollo described his relationship with his son: "The little orphan is always at my side and I can never get rid of my anxiety about him.... I shield him from the atmosphere of this place, and the child grows up as though in a monk's cell." (Gerard, 37) Apollo didn't want his son to go to school in a place seeped in hostility toward Poles. He wanted to raise his son in a Polish environment, not Russian, even if this meant isolation.

Apollo's health grew worse each day, and finally, the governor of Chernikov, witnessing the severity of Apollo's illness, released him from exile. Conrad and his father moved to Cracow in Poland. At this point, Apollo was quite ill with tuberculosis, and also extremely defeated and depressed. The release from exile could not free him from his emotional and physical anguish, and Apollo died four years after Eva. Several thousand people turned out for the funeral, with the young Conrad leading the patriotic procession. Although Conrad would reject much of his father's political passions and turn away from his hope for Conrad to "Be a Pole!," his father's personality and his mood also had a profound affect on Conrad.

The orphan Conrad became the ward of his mother's brother, Tadeusz Bobrowski. His kind, and also very practical, uncle believed that his sister's husband had been a reckless idealist. Tadeusz differed from Apollo in almost every possible way. He wasn't involved in revolutions, and held a passive view on the Polish situation, hoping logic and patience could overcome the Russian stronghold. Unlike Apollo, Tadeusz owned land, and on which grew wheat and sugar beets.

Although legally Conrad was his uncle's ward, he spent most of his time under the care of his maternal grandmother, Teofila Bobrowska, and living in Cracow. From the time of birth until he left Poland as a teenager, he moved around often, living in at least ten different places. Conrad often changed schools and classmates, never forming close friendships with other children, and he attended school sporadically. He did not perform well, disliking the structure and regiment of the education. However, he continued to read extensively on his own.

Conrad was fourteen-years-old when he first announced that he wanted to go to sea. The only subject in school he liked and excelled in was geography, and throughout his childhood he had read many sea adventure books. He believed the sea offered escape, providing open spaces and the freedom he never had during childhood. His family was shocked by this announcement, and tried their best to dissuade Conrad. They sent him on a trip to Switzerland with his tutor, hoping the young man could talk the boy out of his fantasy. Instead, the two argued passionately, and when the frustrated tutor called Conrad "an incorrigible, hopeless Don Quixote," the image surprised and delighted Conrad even more—arousing his romantic notions. (Conrad, 44).

Conrad could not be talked out of his desire to become a sailor. In addition to craving adventure, Conrad needed to leave Poland for practical reasons. As a Russian subject and the son of a deported political convict, Conrad was liable to twenty-five years of military service with the Russian Army. Furthermore, Conrad could not see a future for Poland—the political situation seemed hopeless. He did not believe that Poland would gain independence, and he desired to live in a free country. He favored going to France, where he knew the language, and where many Poles had emigrated. Reluctantly, his uncle gave him his blessing in joining the French merchant navy. In 1874, Conrad, not yet seventeen, quit attending school, and departed for the bustling seaport of Marseilles.

OUT TO SEA

Conrad arrived in Marseilles with two letters of introduction, money from his uncle, and a contact with a small sea vessel company owned by the Delestangs. Away from his home country, Conrad's health and spirits quickly improved. He spent time at the ports conversing with sailors and meeting artists in the many cafes that lined the streets. He tried to learn by observation the lives of the sailors. He enjoyed living in a free country, and away from the burdens of his past. He began sailing on pilot boats, which guided ships into the harbor, and adapted quickly to the sea life. He was impressed with the sailors' way of life and their knowledge of the vast sea. Two months after his arrival, Conrad sailed on one of Delestangs' ships, the *Mont-Blanc*, as a passenger and then an apprentice, making two voyages to the West Indies, and officially beginning his training as a sailor.

For his third trip several months later, Conrad sailed on the schooner *Saint-Antoine* as a steward, this time receiving payment. He spent a short time on the coasts of South America, a setting that would appear in his novel *Nostromo*. On this trip he met first-mate Dominic Cervoni, an experienced and rugged sailor who impressed Conrad with his bold, nomadic personality. Cervoni embodied Conrad's romantic ideals about what a sailor should be—wanderer and adventurer. Later, characters based on Cervoni would appear in several of Conrad's books.

After returning to France, Conrad spent nearly a year on shore, where he partook in the lively environment of the city. Marseilles was filled with theaters, cafes, and rich food and wine. He had his first taste of opera, and fell in love with the art. The culture here differed completely from the sad, isolating environment he had grown up in. Conrad spent his money freely, participating in freedoms he had not been exposed to in his home country. His friends included Royalists, seamen, and bohemians, representing the different aspects of his own personality—aristocrat, sailor, and eventually, writer.

He quickly began to overspend the allowance that his uncle sent him, and in response, Tadeusz wrote ongoing letters to Conrad admonishing his extravagances:

> I learned ... that you had drawn from the Bank in one sum your allowance for the eight months from January till October of that year, and having lent it (or possibly squandered it) you are in need. Subsequently in May, you wrote to me apologizing but not offering any clear explanation. (Sherry, 21).

The troubles with money that were just now beginning would follow Conrad throughout his life. When he had money he spent it, and when he didn't, he borrowed and took loans, and then quickly spent those loans. Tadeusz complained that Conrad was too much like his father, "by your disorder and the easy way you take things—in which you remind me of the Korzeniowski family—spoiling and wasting everything." (Watt, 28) Tadeusz, whose own wife and daughter were dead, had became a surrogate father to Conrad. He cared for his nephew deeply, yet felt frustrated and disappointed in Conrad's carelessness. He didn't feel that Conrad was seriously committed to his career choice, and that he had missed opportunities to advance himself.

Conrad's life began to spiral out of control. He quarreled with Delestang, and considered moving to another country, in hopes of earning more money. He joined the Carlists, who were seeking to seize the throne of Spain for Carlos de Bourbon, and was involved with Cervoni in gun-running adventures to Spain. The dangerous enterprise appealed to Conrad's adolescent ideals of adventure, but the quest soon ended with the ship being sunk to avoid capture, and a loss of more money. Although he made an attempt to return to sailing, the French military wouldn't allow him because he didn't have a permit from the Russian consul releasing him from Russian military duty.

Conrad then invested in a scheme involving contraband, and lost 3000 francs. He borrowed more money from a friend, and squandered that too. This way of life was leading Conrad down a path of destruction. The final blow came when Conrad was injured by a gunshot wound, the cause of which is speculated upon to this day. According to Conrad, he was in a duel over a woman he loved; in Tadeusz's version, Conrad had squandered away the last of his money and then in an act of desperation, shot himself in the chest. Tadeusz wrote, "You were idling for nearly a whole year—you fell into debt, you deliberately shot yourself." (Sherry, 25). Biographers have argued about the identity of the woman who caused the duel, Rita de Lastaola, or if she even existed, or whether Conrad had an affair with her. This woman is credited to have been the model for his book, *The Arrow of Gold*. When referring to the past in his memoirs and novels, Conrad often obscured incidents, and biographers have often had trouble researching the events of his life. He often exaggerated incidents, or even changed the occurrences altogether, raising many questions about his life. Whether or not he was involved with Rita, Conrad's version that his injury resulted from a duel cannot be accounted for, and most Conrad scholars and historians believe that Tadeusz's version is correct—that Conrad had reached the end of the line and committed a desperate, perilous act. Tadeusz journeyed to Marseilles to rescue his nephew—caring for him, paying off his debts, and resolving his doctor bills and rent.

Something needed to change for Conrad. Although he had found freedom to escape from the sad years of his childhood, he also lacked direction in life. While in France, Conrad had participated in a few adventures, but he had also wasted a large amount of money and had not made exceptional progress in his sea-faring career. So, after four years, he decided to leave Marseilles and headed to England and the largest merchant fleet in the world.

BECOMING ENGLISH

When twenty-year-old Joseph Conrad arrived in England, he didn't know a single person, and he barely spoke a word of English. This time he had no contacts, no letters of introduction. He spent the beginning months on coastal voyages, listening to his shipmates and attempting to pick up on the English language. He made several short trips around the British isles on schooners, and then went to London to search for a job on an ocean-sailing berth. He arrived at the city with a map in hand, knowing not one soul, and feeling overwhelmed by all the people. He paid a steep premium to an agent who arranged a term as an unofficial apprentice, allowing him to go on two long voyages to Australia and the Orient, one trip on a wooden clipper, or sailing ship, and the other on a steamer. These trips truly introduced him to the realistic world of sailing.

Although later he sometimes idealized these youthful years, the sailing life was nothing like the way the young, romantic Conrad had envisioned it. Food could become tainted or scarce. Often the living quarters were overcrowded and damp, offering no privacy or solitude. The work was exhausting, tedious, and often dangerous, trying Conrad's already fragile health. Furthermore, the jobs did not pay very much, and they were not easy to come by. More steamers were being used instead of sailing ships, and the number of commanding positions were dwindling. Conrad didn't have an interest in the steamers, and he typically looked for work on the sailing ships. He often developed new schemes to earn money, such as becoming involved in whaling or investing in a business venture, none of which panned out. He wrote in a letter: "It is not the desire of getting much money that prompts me. It is simply the wish to work for myself. I am sick and tired of sailing about for little money and less consideration." (Meyers, 55) However, despite this complaint and all of the hardships, Conrad continued to be drawn to the sea life—he did not want to give up his chosen profession. Against everyone else's wishes and advice, he followed through with this decision, and made the seemingly unthinkable a reality: Joseph Conrad, sailor.

However, Conrad's temperamental personality often interfered with his sailing career. For example, he often quarreled with captains, and hence, never stayed very long with one ship. In his twenty years of sailing, he would work on eighteen different vessels. Instead of sustaining a career with one shipping line, he quit jobs abruptly, and then had difficulty securing a new position. In the tradition that would follow him, he also continued to be unpredictable with money. There were also periods of poor health, idleness, and loneliness. In England, he didn't feel the same kind of ease he had in Marseilles; he felt like a stranger and remained isolated. Even as he learned the language, he still felt like an outsider, and most people viewed him as such.

He did happen to make two close friends during this time, G.F.W. Hope and Adolf Krieger. Hope was a former sailor and now the director of a mercantile company, and Krieger was a partner in a shipping agents firm. Krieger often lent Conrad money, and later the two would have a falling out over a debt Conrad had incurred. However, for a substantial time, these two friendships prevailed, even in later years, after Conrad was coming into contact with important writers and developing literary friendships.

Despite these new friends, the time between jobs that he spent on shore was long and often lonely. He lived in sailors' hostels or lodging houses in remote parts of England, and spent most of the time alone, reading, and writing letters. He continued to correspond regularly with his uncle. Tadeusz now felt that Conrad was becoming more responsible. However, he still worried about him, and urged him to try to stay with one company. Conrad arranged to meet with Tadeusz in Marienbad and then Bohemia, south of Dresden, which gave Conrad a chance to catch up on the news of his friends and family, and to speak in his native language. This was a relaxing and rejuvenating experience for

Conrad, providing him the time he needed away from the sea and the squalid hostels he had grown accustomed to living in.

Over the years Conrad embarked on several voyages to places such as Singapore and Australia. On one particular journey, he was aboard the *Palestine* bound for Bangkok. The ship, old and rusted, was delayed for various repairs. When it set sail, the coal cargo caught on fire and exploded; the ship went up in flames, blowing up the decks and singing and burning the crew. They abandoned the ship, and then it sunk head first. Conrad would later vividly recall this experience in his 1898 short-story "Youth." He also sailed on the *Narcissus* from Bombay to England, the ship and the crew appearing later in his novel, *The Nigger of the "Narcissus."*

Although English ships employed many foreigners, most foreign sailors didn't strive to become officers. However, Conrad was steadily learning English, teaching himself to read and speak the language, and he passed his required set of sea examinations, including his master's certificate exam, allowing him to be hired as a captain. The exam required extensive knowledge of winds, currents, navigation, instruments, and measurements. Conrad also became naturalized as a British citizen, releasing him from Russian citizenship. During this time he wrote his first short story and submitted it unsuccessfully to a contest that called for stories about sailing life. At this point, he had no desire to be a writer; he was a sea merchant, what he had dreamed about as a young boy. His uncle urged him to record his sea adventures and send them to a Warsaw; weekly, however, Conrad ignored this advice, and did no other writing except for letters.

Even as an English citizen, Conrad was still considered an alien, and jobs were hard to come by. Now that he was nearly thirty years old, the age at which his uncle's allowance would be cut off, Conrad needed to try to find steady work. He signed on as first mate on the *Highland Forest*, bound for Samarang in Java. On this voyage the ship rolled and jerked, and Conrad was hit in the back by a flying spar, causing him to check into a hospital in Singapore. The first time he saw Singapore, he was amazed by the activity and people, and the vibrant setting of the Eastern port and the many people he met there would later inspire several novels.

After being discharged from the hospital, Conrad decided that he would sign on as first mate on the *Vider*, instead of returning to England. The 800-ton steamer ship made several voyages between Singapore and

Borneo, stopping at trading posts. According to Jean-Aubry in *The Sea Dreamer*, Conrad became friendly with the captain, soaking up all the stories the captain could tell, and intensely observed the places and people he came into contact with. (Jean-Aubrey, 124) The steamer hit bad weather, heavy rain and thunderstorms, and Conrad changed the course of the ship just in time, thus escaping the upcoming rocks that certainly would have wrecked the ship. When the steamer went upriver to Borneo, Conrad first met the strange and much talked about trader Charles Olmeijer, whose contradictory life—dressed in pajamas, but infamous for his grand ambitions—would inspire Conrad's first novel.

A year later Conrad secured a position as captain on the small steamer, the *Otago*, after the original captain died during the previous voyage. Conrad always remembered this voyage with affection as "my first command ... sure of a tenderly remembered existence as long as I live." (Sherry, 25) Yet Conrad often romanticized the truth of his sailing years. In reality, the voyage to Singapore took three weeks instead of the usual few days because of lack of wind, and much of his crew being ill with fever, dysentery, and cholera. Furthermore, Conrad wasn't popular with his mates. Although Conrad could often be overly loquacious and filled with flattery when he liked a person, most of the time he was aloof, and people often thought him strange. Polite, but overly formal, Conrad didn't fit in with the other sailors. His Polish background, noble-gentry heritage, mannerly way of speaking, and intellectual activity set him apart from the other sailors.

He also did not look like the other sailors, and this definitely pushed him to the outside. By most accounts, Conrad didn't reach over 5'6", the most memorable feature being his dark, penetrating eyes, and he dressed in an elegant manner, very much aware of his Polish heritage. One French charterer described Conrad as "always dressed like a fop [*petit maître*] ... in a dark jacket, usually a light-coloured waistcoat, and a fancy pair of trousers, all of these well made and of great elegance; he wore a black or grey bowler hat slightly to one side, always had gloves on and carried a gold-headed Malacca cane." (Watt, 19) People remembered him as dressing like a dandy. He was a Pole in English attire, perhaps hoping to look like an English gentleman, while living the life of a sailor.

Although he had outgrown the epilepsy of his childhood, Conrad was still a nervous, high-strung man, described as having "a tick of the shoulder and of the eyes, and the most minor unexpected occurrence—

something falling on the floor or a door slamming—would make him jump." (Watt, 24) In addition, Conrad's heavy accent also distanced him from the other sailors. He had learned to speak English, but often people had trouble understanding his broken words and strong Polish accent.

Again, somewhat abruptly, Conrad resigned from this command position after several months. He returned to England and lived leisurely, wandering the streets of London. He rented a place in North London, not far from the Thames. Although he worked for a short time at a firm of shipping agents, he spent most of time relaxing, roaming the streets, sometimes meeting with his friend Adolf Krieger, and asking around for a berth to command.

Then, one autumn morning after breakfast, he asked the landlord's daughter to clear his table, a change from his usual habit to dally over his breakfast. Once she left, he sat at the table there for some time, staring out the window. Then he put down his pipe, and he picked up a pen.

"Never did a writer's life begin so late or so casually," states Jean-Aubry. (Jean-Aubry, 151) Conrad was thirty-two years old. He claimed he had no plan to begin writing a novel, that the moment had just happened: "The conception of a planned book was entirely outside my mental range when I sat down to write; the ambition of being an author had never turned up amongst these gracious imaginary existences one creates fondly for oneself...." (Conrad, 13) While it was true that Conrad had not written anything except letters and one short story, he certainly had the literary background and history to point him in this direction.

Interestingly, Conrad chose not to write in Polish or French, but in English, his third learned language. Polish was the language of his childhood and homeland, which he had deserted, and it did not feel right to use this language. He knew French, but used it as a language to express elegance—it could not serve the stories he wanted to write. It was English that he was using daily, and English also represented his mature self—the person he had constructed over the years. He had learned conversational English from the sailors, studied the newspaper to learn the basics of the written language, and then read Shakespeare for poetic and literary language. Conrad did not even hesitate about which language to use: "When I wrote the first words of *Almayer's Folly*, I had already been *thinking* in English." (Watt, 22) It was this fine morning that Conrad started to write his first novel, based on the trader he had met in Borneo while sailing the *Vider*.

CONGO

Although he had officially started writing his first novel and moving toward the track of becoming a writer, Conrad had certainly not given up the sailing life. He still saw himself as a sailor, not a writer. After time on shore, he was eager to go back to the sea. For months he searched unsuccessfully for a commanding position on a ship—nothing was available. Frustrated, he became enticed by the idea of journeying to the Congo; the thought of sailing to Africa awakened in Conrad the passions of his childhood. He had read all of the explorer novels, and his ideas of journeying to Africa were colored by exciting tales of heroism and discovery. As a child, his favorite subject had been geography, and he recalls in *A Personal Record* that at nine or ten years old he had pointed to a map of Africa, telling himself, "When I grow up I shall go *there*." (Conrad, 13)

The publicity over more recent African adventures also fueled his desire to go. For example, British explorer and journalist Henry Morton Stanley had discovered Dr. Livingstone in the center of the continent, and the Congo, the private property of King Leopold II, now present-day Zaire, was very much in the public eye during the late nineteenth century. Explorers and adventurers eager to "bring civilization" to Africa sailed to the Congo, and trading posts were being established all across Central Africa. The voyage offered danger, excitement, and adventure, and Conrad was ready for something new. Alfred Krieger's firm connected Conrad to ship brokers, and he interviewed with them in Brussels. They gave him the impression that they might have a position for him, although couldn't tell him anything definite.

A few months after he interviewed, Conrad followed through with his original plans to go back to Poland to visit his uncle. Now that he was a British citizen, he could return to his home country without problems. Conrad had finally secured a visa, and would be able to return to Poland, without troubles from Russian authorities. He had not been back since he left sixteen years ago as a young man.

Before he made the trip, his uncle put him in touch with a distant cousin, Alexander Poradowski, who lived in Brussels. Conrad hoped that perhaps this relative would have connections that could help him secure his appointment with the ship brokers in Brussels. However, Alexander was ill, and actually died two days after Conrad arrived to visit.

Alexander's wife, French-born Marguerite Poradowska, and Conrad were drawn together in wake of this tragedy. She offered to help him in any way she could. Conrad fondly called Marguerite "Aunt," although the two were related only by her marriage to his distant cousin. Marguerite was an intelligent, cultured, beautiful, and sophisticated woman, nine years older than Conrad. She was also a novelist. When Conrad said good-bye he took a copy of her first novel with him.

Conrad continued on his journey to Poland, traveling to his uncle's estate in Kiev. For two months he visited with friends and family, spending most his time with Tadeusz. His uncle was happy to see Conrad, but he also presented him with a full documentation of Conrad's expenses, since he first departed Poland: "*Thus the making of a man out of Mr Konrad has cost*—apart from the 3,600 roubles given you as capital—17,454 roubles." (Sherry, 55) Although Tadeusz was not pleased with Conrad's decision to go to Africa, he could see the change in his nephew—since his wilder days in Marseilles, he had become more responsible, and he seemed quite dedicated to his life as a sailor.

When Conrad returned to Brussels, he found that he was needed immediately to travel to the Congo. One of the captains had been murdered, and Conrad was hired to replace the dead captain of a steamer in the Congo—just in the same manner he had been hired to captain the *Otago*. The captain's death wasn't the only reason Conrad was hired—his "aunt" Marguerite had used her influence to connect him to the right people. Now, he was about to follow his childhood dream of traveling to Africa. Thirty-two years old, Conrad signed a three-year contract, his longest yet, and he embarked for the Congo, taking his novel manuscript along with him.

He departed from Bordeaux and traveled along the west coast of Africa. After a month long voyage, he arrived in Boma, the capital, on June 12, 1890, then took a small steamer forty miles up on the lower Congo to Matadi. For the first time, Conrad started keeping a diary, after his uncle and Marguerite had been urging him to take notes on his voyages. In Africa, Conrad recorded his impressions of the environment and people of the great continent. Conrad quickly realized he didn't get along with the other sailors and white travelers, who had come to Congo for one basic mission—money.

In Matadi he met Roger Casement, the only white person on the trip whom he actually liked and respected. Casement would later receive recognition for exposing the terrible atrocities being committed in the Congo, and revealing that Leopold was a tyrant. While Leopold controlled the Congo, the Belgians forced many of the native people into slavery. Ivory was the most valuable commodity, and people were demoralized, humiliated, and killed for it. Once Casement arrived and witnessed what was happening, he quickly began to question the idea of Western progress and European enlightenment, a questioning which would also take root in Conrad's own writing, as he explored the dark nature of human beings.

From Matadi, Conrad had to reach Kinshasa. The stretch was not navigable by river, and the railway wasn't yet completed. With no other alternative, Conrad traveled this 230-mile passage by foot, an eighteen-day trip. This stretch of time left deep impressions on Conrad, images that he could not forget, and would reappear in one of his most admired books, *Heart of Darkness*. The days were hot and sticky, thick with mosquitoes, and the nights were cold and dreary. His traveling companion was sick with fever, and drinking water was tainted. The journey was dangerous and foreboding—while on the way, Conrad passed a skeleton tied to a post and also noticed a rotting corpse. He documented the grueling days and described the horror in his diary, which he wrote in English. Even when he didn't write something down, the details still stayed with him, burned into his memory.

When he arrived to Kinshasa, after the long, risky, and exhausting trip, he had his first hostile meeting with his superior, Camille Delcommune. The manager was irritated that Conrad's trip had taken so long, and then he informed him that the ship he was supposed to command was damaged. So Conrad boarded another steamer, the *Roi des Belges*, but not as the captain. The ship sailed upriver stopping at various trading posts to Stanley Falls. Conrad's journey was not the romantic adventurism he had once imagined.

On the trip upriver he witnessed the atrocities the "civilized" whites committed against the native people; he observed the greed for ivory and the brutal exploitation of resources and people.

Fever and dysentery were prevalent in Stanley Falls, and much of the crew became sick, including the captain of the *Roi des Belges*. So for a few days Conrad commanded the ship, until the captain recovered. When the ship returned to Kinshasa, Conrad also fell gravely ill with dysentery and malarial fever. His poor health only increased his animosity toward the insensitive Delcommune. The two continued to quarrel, and Conrad realized that Delcommune was not going to give him the command he had been promised. He developed a deep resentment for Delcommune, calling him "a common ivory dealer with base instincts."

A letter he wrote to Marguerite depicted the deploring conditions and his overall attitude toward the journey:

> Decidedly I regret having come here. I even regret it bitterly.... Everything here is repellent to me. Men and things, but men above all. And I am repellent to them, also. From the manager in Africa who has taken the trouble to tell one and all that I offend him supremely, down to the lowest mechanic, they all have the gift of irritating my nerves.... I cannot look forward to anything because I don't have a ship to command. (Karl and Davies, eds., 62)

Conrad wished he had never made the ill-fated trip, and now wanted desperately to leave the Congo for good. He could no longer endure the situation, and he decided to return home, breaking his contract—something that the majority of sailors did after they witnessed the disease and horrors of the journey. He made the trip back to Matadi, ill and exhausted.

After only serving for six months, Conrad sailed back to England, appearing close to death, overcome with fever and psychological exhaustion. Alfred Krieger, seeing how sick Conrad was, arranged for him to enter the hospital in London. From there he went to a spa near Geneva for a water cure, and he slowly recovered. While in recuperation, he returned to what he had started before he ever left for the Congo—his novel. He completed the eighth chapter of *Almayer's Folly*, then returned to London.

To make money, he worked again for the shipping company, running the warehouse for a short time, but he was desperately unhappy, overcome by a gloomy darkness which lasted most of the year. He wrote to Marguerite Poradowska: "I am still plunged in deepest night, and my dreams are only nightmares." (Sherry, 63). Conrad's adventure to the Congo affected him immensely; what he had witnessed there could never be erased from his conscious. His view of humanity grew even more somber. The malarial fever he contracted in the Congo ruined his health, but even more influential than the physical ailments were the psychological effects of the journey. Back on shore, he continued to work on and off on his novel, the same one he had started before the Congo, but he often fell into depression. His letters during this time were filled with dark, despairing reflections on humankind. However, even though he had no desire to ever go back to Africa, the trip to the Congo had not diminished Conrad's deep connection to the sea life.

BECOMING A WRITER

Despite his continuous health problems and nightmarish memories of the Congo, Conrad again craved the adventurous nautical lifestyle. He had recovered as much as he could from the journey to the Congo, and now he was looking for something new. He'd grown restless with the novel, and desired the setting of the sea. It took him fourteen months to find a new berth. Then, an old acquaintance secured Conrad a chief mate position on the *Torrens*, one of the fastest clippers of its time and the most famous ship he ever sailed on.

On the ship's first voyage Conrad became friendly with one of the passengers, W.H. Jacques, who had come from Cambridge and was traveling to recuperate, as he was ill with tuberculosis. The two discussed literature and loaned each other books, and one day Conrad, on a sudden impulse, handed Jacques the first nine chapters of his unfinished novel to read. For three years, the manuscript had traveled around with him, even to the Congo (where he'd almost lost it), and Conrad had never showed it to anyone. He recounts in *A Personal Record* how the next day he asked Jaques if he thought the novel was worth finishing, and he replied, "Distinctly." (Conrad, 17) Jacques encouraged him to finish the novel, and this was exactly the kind of positive reinforcement that Conrad needed.

On the second voyage on the *Torrens*, Conrad met two young passengers who had been educated at Harrow and Oxford, Ted Sanderson, son of the headmaster of Elstree Preparatory School, and the future writer John Galsworthy, both who became lifelong friends of his. Galsworthy described Conrad: "The first mate is a Pole called Conrad and is a capital chap, though queer to look at; he is a man of travel and experience in many parts of the world, and has a fund of yarns on which

I draw freely." (Meyers, 112) Conrad, drawn to the more educated, literary passengers, felt he had more common with them than he did with the crew. Conrad never mentioned he was writing a novel, but instead he entertained Sanderson and Galsworthy with tales of his sea adventures. They grew close during the fifty-six days on board, building strong friendships.

During this same time, Conrad's letters to Marguerite indicated that perhaps he was growing tired of the sea. He called his occupation a "uniform grey of existence." (Karl, 125) Although these trips were pleasant and the *Torrens* was an impressive ship, Conrad had now been sailing on and off for nearly twenty years and he abruptly left the *Torrens* to visit his uncle in Poland for a month. Tadeusz cared for Conrad, whose health continued to be unstable: "my uncle looks after me like a boy." (Sherry, 65) Tadeusz felt relieved that Conrad was now an English citizen, and he also felt proud that he had risen through the ranks of seamen.

It then took Conrad another thirteen months to find a berth, and during this time he fell into a depression. "It seems to me I have seen nothing, see nothing, and shall always see nothing. I could swear there is only the void outside the walls of the room where I am writing these lines," he wrote to Marguerite. (Karl, 131) Days passed slowly. Still, he searched for work. Sailing ships were becoming more and more difficult to secure as steamers were becoming more available. Although Conrad continued to prefer the sailing vessels, he also knew he had to take whatever work he could find. So he accepted a lower position on a steamer, the *Adowa*, but this ship never set sail. Conrad spent six weeks aboard the moored ship. During this time he people-watched and spent a lot of time thinking, and also wrote letters to Marguerite.

Conrad and Marguerite had grown close. They wrote each other hundreds of letters. She sent him her stories and novels, and he replied with flattering, complimentary letters. He could clearly see her future as a writer, but not his own. While Conrad had been sailing he had also been reading, and corresponding with her about literature. For example, *Madam Bovary* had a strong influence on Conrad, and he greatly admired Flaubert's style. He told Marguerite: "One never questions for a moment either his characters or his incidents, one would rather doubt one's own existence." (Meyers, 118) Although Conrad liked to give the idea that he became a writer by accident, these threads of his life were beginning to tie together: he had come from a literary family, he read voraciously most of his life, and he corresponded with Marguerite often about the styles, influences, and techniques of literature.

After the *Adowa's* trip was officially cancelled, Conrad returned to London. Then in January, 1894, ten days after he left the *Adowa*, he received the devastating news that his uncle Tadeusz was dead. The news shattered Conrad. The nephew and uncle had written each other letters continuously ever since Conrad left Poland as a young man. "It seemed as if everything has died in me," Conrad told Marguerite. "He seems to have carried my soul away with him." (Karl, 148) The last time Conrad saw him was during his month long trip to Poland, when his uncle had cared for him.

Isolated, and still mourning his uncle, Conrad worked on his novel, which grew slowly, line by line. Writing was tedious; he often stared at the blank page and became discouraged and frustrated. But he also felt like he couldn't leave the desk, because sometimes in those moments of gazing into space, ideas would come to him. He wrote to Marguerite, "If I let go, I am lost! I am writing to you just as I go out. I must indeed go out sometimes, alas! I begrudge each minute I spend away from the page. I do not say from the pen, for I have written very little, but inspiration comes to me while gazing at the paper." (Karl, 151)

During this period of his life, Conrad depended very much on Marguerite's advice and support. They became more intimate with their letters. However, Marguerite could not replace Tadeusz, and Conrad missed his uncle immensely. Tadeusz's death also symbolized something else—the loss of his childhood home. Conrad had emigrated from his home country, the place his father had fought so passionately for, and now his main ties to that place were cut. He felt unsettled, and lonely.

However distraught and lonely Conrad was after the death of his uncle, he summoned enough energy to finish *Almayer's Folly*. He'd spent five years on and off working on the book, and now it was completed. He dedicated the novel to his deceased uncle.

Conrad sent the manuscript to the publisher Fisher Unwin, but he didn't feel very confident in his own writing. He came up with various, far-fetched ideas, perhaps to cushion possible rejection. For example, he thought about having Marguerite translating the book into French and calling the book a collaboration project with her, or even naming her the sole author of the book, but Marguerite refused to take part in this scheme. He told her, "This may go on for months, and in the end, I don't think they will accept it." (Sherry, 68) While waiting for news on his book, Conrad was also negotiating for various ships. When he didn't get a quick reply from the publisher, the anxious, nerve-wracked Conrad wrote to them and asked for the manuscript to be returned.

However, four months after Conrad had submitted *Almayer's Folly*, the book was accepted. A young reader for the company, Edward Garnett, had recommended the book for publication. Garnett recognized this writer's talent and potential. He was curious to meet the author, and so the two had lunch. Garnett observed Conrad was "short but extremely graceful in his nervous gestures, with brilliant eyes, now narrow and penetrating, now soft and warm ... whose speech was ingratiating, guarded or brusk turn by turn." (Meyers, 121) When Garnett casually referred to Conrad's next book, Conrad sat back in his chair and announced, "I don't expect to write again. It is likely I shall soon be going to sea."(Watt, 68) However, Garnett encouraged Conrad to write more, assuring him his first book was very good, so "why not write another?" After this inspiring talk, when Conrad returned to his lodgings, he wrote half a page of what would be his next novel. He now was committed to another book, and although he didn't know it yet, another life. Conrad had been a sailor for twenty years, but he would never return to the sea; with the publication of his novel, his life was now changing dramatically.

ADJUSTING TO LIFE ON LAND

Fisher Unwin had given Conrad an advance for a second book. Like his first novel, this one had a Malayan setting, contains some of the same characters, and resonates with themes of isolation and loneliness.

Conrad was writing regularly; however, the words did not come easily and he found his work to be difficult and exhausting. He complained, "Ideas don't come. I don't see either the characters or the events." (Jean-Aubry, 205) Conrad again felt restless, maybe in part because of the difficulty he was having with his writing. He thought returning to the sea would settle him. So while he was working on the book, he was also in the midst of actively looking for a job. He wrote, "My work is not getting on and my health is gone. If I stay ashore much longer, everything will be ruined." (Jean-Aubry, 205) After traveling by sea for twenty years, he felt uneasy on land. He didn't believe that his sailing career was finished for good. To add to his struggle with his writing, health problems affected Conrad on and off, especially attacks of the gout, which had infected him in the Congo. Gout causes acute inflammatory arthritis in the joints, and at the time, there were no drugs to cure the disease. The physical effects were closely linked with the psychological for Conrad: the more anxious he felt, the more likely the gout was to return; likewise, the gout attacks intensified his anxiety.

In 1895, *Almayer's Folly* appeared in print, with his long Polish name shortened to Joseph Conrad, which he had started calling himself after all the mispronunciations and misspellings of his name in England. Critics reacted favorably to the novel, in both England and America. Even with this kind of critical praise, Conrad doubted his writing abilities. He was staying in close touch with Garnett, sending him chapters of his new novel-in-progress. He was nervous about the outcome of *Outcast of the Islands*, and Garnett, an important literary figure in Conrad's life, responded with support and enthusiasm. The two friends exchanged ideas, suggestions, questions and advice. Garnett provided Conrad with the friendship, frank criticism, and encouragement that he needed, and he was a major part of his life for many years.

That same year, Conrad decided to go to Champel, Switzerland for recuperation of his health and nerves, and while there he finished nearly a third of his book. During this recovery, the writing came with more ease, and he completed a substantial part of the novel. When he returned to London, he spent the summer yachting with his old friend, G.F.W. Hope. He started another project, "The Sisters," a romance involving a Ukrainian painter; however, Garnett encouraged him to abandon it.

Conrad had been a loner for most of his life. The isolation started in childhood, and continued through his lonely nights at sea. However, his solitary life was about to change. A year after he finished *Outcast of Islands*, Conrad married Jessie Emmeline George.

Although Conrad had courted a few women in Europe and England, and was possibly rejected by several of these women, he did not have much romantic experience. He had not participated in the typical sailor lifestyle of visiting prostitutes at the ports. One of his most intimate contacts with a woman consisted of the letters he wrote to

Marguerite. It is possible the two distant relatives felt connected to each other, but their age difference and backgrounds kept them apart. Once he started courting Jessie, the letters between Conrad and Marguerite broke off for several years. He was also involved in a close relationship with another young woman, Mlle. Emilie Briquel, whom he had met at Champel. However, it was his unexpected friendship with Jessie that prevailed.

Conrad had met Jessie through his friend Hope, some time between 1893 and 1894, and a friendship developed, even though their backgrounds and interests were completely different. Jessie came from a large working-class London family, and was working as a typist when they met. She wasn't sophisticated or formally educated like the other women Conrad had admired, such as Marguerite, and she was sixteen years younger than Conrad.

By now, Conrad looked a little more like a sailor (except he still dressed with his overcoat and bowler hat)—he had grown a nautical beard, and his face was weathered and rough—and he must have seemed unusual to Jessie, even exciting. His marriage proposal was typical of Conrad's nervous and often brusque manner. They were taking shelter from a storm at the National Gallery, when he blurted out, "Look here, my dear, we had better get married and get out of this. Look at the weather. We will get married at once and get over to France. How soon can you be ready? In a week—a fortnight?" (Meyers, 137) He then later told her the reason for his impatience was that he didn't have very long to live, and also informed her he had no intention of having children. After this abrupt, startling proposal, Jessie didn't hear from Conrad for three days, and she wondered if he were actually serious about marriage.

Garnett tried to dissuade Conrad from the marriage, believing that Jessie was not right for him and that the two did not have enough in common. He reasoned that Conrad would be miserable because Jessie came from a different background and did not have the same intellectual pursuits. However, Conrad, who was approaching forty, had begun to wish for the security of marriage. He'd wanted to settle down from the sailing life. He felt comfortable around Jessie, and did not fear rejection with her.

After they were married they spent about six months on the coast of Brittany for their honeymoon, and Conrad was quite pleased by the location and the large house. However, much of the time was tarnished by illness, anxiety, and lack of money, all characteristics that would continue throughout their marriage. Jessie became Conrad's typist, and she also had to care for him while he was ill—which in the beginning she found overwhelming and disturbing: "To see him lying in the white canopied bed, dark-faced, with gleaming teeth and shining eyes, was sufficiently alarming, but to hear him muttering to himself a strange tongue (he must have been speaking Polish), to be unable to penetrate the clouded mind or catch one intelligible word, was for a young, inexperienced girl truly awful." (Sherry, 72) Jessie had left behind her family and home, and traveled to a place where she did not know the language, with a nervous, irritable husband. However, after the initial shock, the two seemed to work out the differences between them. In many ways, they complemented each other. Jessie's calm temperament eased Conrad's high-strung, passionate, and overly-sensitive personality.

While on the island, Conrad worked on a new novel about the sea, *The Rescue*, but he soon became frustrated with the manuscript, partly stemming from his physical battle with terrible attacks of gout. He fell into fits of depression, and lamented to Garnett his trouble: "I have long fits of depression, that in a lunatic asylum would be called madness." (Karl, 284) Two months later he wrote,

> "When I face that fatal manuscript it seems to me that I have forgotten how to think—worse! how to write. It is as if something in my head had given way to let in a cold grey mist. I knock about blindly in it till I am positively, physically sick—and then I give up saying—tomorrow! And tomorrow comes—and brings only the renewed and futile agony. I ask myself whether I am breaking up mentally. I am afraid of it." (Karl, 296)

The writing took all of his energy; nothing would flow. To make matters worse, he lost a substantial amount of money—his large inheritance from Uncle Tadeusz—in South African gold mines that he had recklessly invested in. Money was scarce, and now he didn't just have himself to think about, but also Jessie.

Unlike his first novel, *An Outcast of the Islands* received mostly mixed and negative reviews. However, one notable reviewer in the *Saturday Review* gave Conrad encouragement, and Conrad wrote the magazine to find out the anonymous reviewer's name. He promptly received a reply from H.G. Wells. This personal response delighted Conrad, and gave him a glimmer of confidence and hope.

Although he could not make substantial progress with the novel, he was able to produce several short stories, writing them quite easily. He wrote "The Idiots," in the style of Maupassant, a story about a mother of several "idiots" who kills her husband to prevent conception of more children, and "An Outpost of Progress" which takes place in the Congo, the story serving as a precursor to *Heart of Darkness*. The time on the island served as a writing apprenticeship for Conrad, and also gave him and Jessie time to establish their relationship and learn more about each other.

IVY WALLS

The damp and cold of the island affected Conrad's susceptible health, and so he and Jessie decided to leave the island and return to England. They moved to an unattractive, small rented house in Stanford-le-Hope, Essex, near the residence of the Hopes. Conrad set to finish a short story that had bloomed into a novel. Wrestling with techniques, language, and style, he never pretended that writing was easy, never made it seem as if he could sit down at his desk and let the words flow. Writing was hard work, and he let others know just how extremely laborious this activity could be for him. He wrote Garnett, "I can't eat.—I dream—nightmares—and scare my wife. I wish it were over!" (Karl, 330). Conrad's melancholic personality seemed to only make the act of writing even more arduous. And, his difficulty with the English language also affected the writing process. He sometimes felt as if he were writing in a language that did not belong to him, and had trouble finding the right phrase, the best description.

His morning routine consisted of eating breakfast, and then retreating to his room to write, composing his works with a pen. However, he usually began slowly, not even starting to write until the afternoon or later. Sometimes he had spurts of writing late at night. Often when he was coming close to the novel's end, he would stay up all hours of the night, until the last word had been written.

Although later he denied taking notes, hoping to give the impression that every book was born solely from his creative mind,

Meyers explains he often took extensive notes from source books in order to refresh his memory of places and people. Usually, his work was inspired both by researching and actual memories, the two aspects coming together to form his imaginative writing. (Meyers, 169) In *A Personal Record*, Conrad explains his philosophy of wanting to recreate these places and people by imagination, and take the reader into this world: "Imagination, not invention, is the supreme master of art as of life." (Conrad, 25) He transformed his experiences from sailing into art. He recreated and imagined these worlds, and brought them to life with his words—which he did tediously, creating his works at a slow pace. He could go a day with only completing several sentences.

In March 1897, after living in the cramped house for five nearly unbearable months, Conrad and Jessie moved not very far away to a fifteenth-century farm house called Ivy Walls. This house was more comfortable and larger, with an attractive landscape and view of the Thames, and Conrad felt happier. He stayed busy writing, interrupted again by vicious attacks of gout. Still terribly blocked on *The Rescue*, he felt like he couldn't abandon the work and continued to face it every day. Exhausted from writing and health problems, he sometimes cruised the Thames on Hope's yacht, the closest he could come to sailing again. His need for money intensified, and the pressure made writing his novel even more difficult. He spent most of his time isolated, and had no real literary contacts.

All of this was about to change. After the short stories he'd written on the island were all published in magazines, and William Ernest Henley's renowned *New Review* serialized the short story cum novel, *The Nigger of the "Narcissus,"* Conrad was soon meeting new people and developing a network of contacts.

He had already met the author he most admired: after sending Henry James a copy of *Outcast of the Islands* with a flattering inscription, James had invited Conrad for lunch to his London flat. Conrad had a reverent, awe-struck attitude toward James's work, and toward the man himself. Conrad's strongest literary influences were Turgenev, Flaubert, and Maupassant, and Henry James had known all of these authors. Conrad felt that James presented sophisticated technical points, and felt that his writing was exquisite and near perfection. Conrad and James became acquaintances, the two foreigners often speaking to each other in French, and with the noticeable politeness that was typical of both of their demeanors. They never, however, established a close friendship.

After reading the serialization of *An Outcast of the Islands* in the *New Review*, a young American writer was captivated by what he read, and requested to his publisher to set up a meeting with Conrad. Stephen Crane, fourteen years younger than Conrad, had already published *Maggie: A Girl of the Streets* and *The Red Badge of Courage*. Crane was quite enthusiastic about Conrad's work, and Conrad was drawn to Crane's adventure-seeking personality, which reminded him of his own in his younger days. The two writers established such a friendly rapport that they did not want to part after lunch. They spent the rest of the evening walking around London and talking about literature, and developed a close friendship until Crane's early death from tuberculosis in 1900.

A month after meeting Crane, Conrad met R.B. Cunninghame Graham, a writer, Scottish aristocrat, and radical member of Parliament, at Graham's request. Graham had read Conrad's short story "An Outpost of Progress" in *Cosmopolis*, and was stirred by Conrad's progressive view on colonialism. Graham also led a daring life, living for eight years in South America, and then searching for gold in Spain. He had spent a good deal of time traveling, and he was extremely political—a democratic aristocrat, radical, and idealist. While Graham was critical of Parliament and more of an anarchist, Conrad was more conservative. However, even though their politics differed, the two developed a very close relationship, exchanging ideas about literature, philosophy, and humanity.

The literary connections were growing. While all of these experienced authors were setting up meetings with him, Conrad was also staying in touch with earlier contacts. For instance, playing a mentor role to John Galsworthy, Conrad was helping him publish his first novel.

Although Conrad had made an impression on important literary figures and was starting to build significant friendships, *The Nigger of the "Narcissus"* was not a success with the general public. Except for sailors and critics, not many people were reading his work. Struggling financially, he hoped to secure more readers, so that he could be more economically stable. The only money he made was from his writing, and this immense pressure contributed to his constant turmoil with writing. At forty, he had hit a ceiling, blocked with his writing and financially desperate. He wrote to Garnett that he had gone "over the rise of forty to travel downwards—and a little more lonely than before." (Watt, 129)

He finished writing stories for his collection, *Tales of the Unrest*, and then tried again unsuccessfully to return to *The Rescue*. Conrad was feeling unsettled and nervous, and when the writing was difficult, he especially longed to return to the sea—something he knew and understood. He hoped to return to those days of adventure and risks, to those days of youth. Then he found out Jessie was pregnant.

He documented his reaction in a letter, "I am not unduly elated." (Meyers, 167) He feared for Jessie's health, and also worried about his dire financial situation with this new addition to the family. Conrad also feared that the new child would take Jessie's attention away from himself. Jessie had somewhat of a maternal relationships with Conrad, fussing over him and taking care of him, and he was highly dependent on her.

The birth of a son certainly did not squelch Conrad's desire to return to the nomadic life he had once led. Shortly after Borys was born, Conrad wrote to Cunninghame Graham, asking for his help in securing a position on a Scottish ship: "To get to sea would be salvation. I am really in a deplorable state, mentally." (Meyers, 172) Graham was actually talking to ship owners and trying to help Conrad find a position, and Conrad naively thought he would bring along his family. However, nothing ensued, and instead of returning to the waves, he stayed at his desk.

Conrad easily became despondent and depressed, and he wrote his most despairing letters to Garnett, with whom he corresponded regularly. He complained of sitting down to write and completing only three sentences in the course of eight hours, and stated, "Pages accumulate and the story stands still. I feel suicidal." (Watt, 130) In addition to his troubles with creativity, as the year drew on, his financial situation also worsened. He borrowed money, and then couldn't pay back the loans. He typically spent more than he earned.

In the entire year of 1898, the only new fiction he completed was a short story, "Youth." However, the story was accepted by a well-paying magazine, *Blackwood's Magazine*, which opened more doors for Conrad. This journal had published many well-known Victorian novelists, and at the time of Conrad's publication, had become more conservative in style and tone. This publication not only helped out financially, but also boosted Conrad's confidence—he was entering his most creative period.

PENT FARM

Conrad, who often blamed his living quarters for his writing blocks and anxiety, began to detest Ivy Walls, where he had made such little progress with his writing. After he met Ford Madox Ford (then called Hueffer), Ford offered to sublet his rented house in Kent, Pent Farm. Conrad liked the place immediately. The house was small and old, lacking electricity and water, but it was intimate and charming. The view of the garden, the hedges hills and hedges that blocked the villages, and the deep green meadows all pleased Conrad. The family moved in the autumn. Pent Farm was remote, yet by chance, it also happened to be at the heart of the literary scene in England.

He now lived in close vicinity to Henry James, Ford Madox Ford, H.G. Wells, and Stephen Crane. John Galsworthy visited often, as did Edward Garnett, and H.G. Wells even brought by George Bernard Shaw. His biographer Jean-Aubry explains that Conrad, "was never at any time in his life in such constant contact with first-class writers." (Jean-Aubrey, 235) Conrad established important connections, and close, long-term friendships evolved.

The levels of friendship varied. For example, Wells and Conrad had a distant relationship, staying in contact with each other, but never developing a close relationship. Conrad continued to stay close friends with Galsworthy and Garnett, yet of this company, Conrad was probably closest to Ford.

Ford Madox Ford had published his first book in his teens; he had many connections to the artistic and literary world of England. Later, he would become a major novelist and editor. Ford and Conrad developed an intimate friendship, often spending working and leisure time together. They admired the same writers, such as James, Flaubert, and Maupassant, and they often conversed in French. Both were anxious and hyper-sensitive men, often irritable, but they got along very well. They visited each other, talking late into the night, and their families joined each other for holidays, although Jessie did not like Ford or his wife Elsie. They often treated her like a servant, and unfortunately, Conrad never stepped in to defend his wife.

Ford liked and respected Conrad, but like many of Conrad's acquaintances, also found him strange, with his strong accent and nervous personality. Ford once ran into him in London and did not recognize him at first, observing an "old, shrunken, wizened man, in an unbrushed bowler, an ancient burst-seamed overcoat, one wrist wrapped in flannel, the other hand helping him to lean on a hazel walking-stick, cut from a hedge and prepared at home. [He] had in one tortured eye a round piece of dirty window-glass." (Meyers, 180) However, whereas other acquaintances of Conrad seemed unable to ever move completely past his foreignness, Ford felt that Conrad was one of his closest friends, and one of the most impressive writers of the period. For his part, Ford was the only one able to inspire and stimulate Conrad in those times when he was ill or exhausted or depressed. He could alleviate Conrad's self-doubt and misery. He abated Conrad's loneliness, and in times of need, loaned him money.

The growth of Conrad's new friendships coincided with the development of his writing career. Slowly, he was beginning to receive more recognition for his writing. His story collection, *Tales of the Unrest*, was awarded a literary prize of fifty guineas from the *Academy*. His published works were receiving praise; people were learning his name— Joseph Conrad, the Pole who now wrote in English, the sailor who was now a writer.

The years at Pent Farm were troubled by poverty, yet greatly inspired with Conrad's hard work. The household revolved around him and his writing—when he was writing, he was not to be disturbed. He could become extremely irritable and irascible, and often ran the household as if he were the captain of a crew. However, Jessie often eased Conrad's quick-temper and continued to give him the attention he needed. Although Conrad could be extremely demanding and self-centered, he also had true affection for Jessie, and enjoyed being in her company. Many of Conrad's new literary friends didn't like Jessie. They found her a "bore," and although usually polite to her face, could be scathing behind her back. Jessie was kind and patient, and Conrad depended on her very much; however, she could not engage in the literary conversations for which he depended upon his new set of friends.

Despite the hardships, his years at Pent Farm proved to be his most productive years. There, he first created Marlow, a narrator of many of his works, and he wrote *Heart of Darkness*, which was considered the second story in a three-story collection, *Youth*. It had been ten years since Conrad journeyed to the Congo, however, the details and memories of the fateful trip had not left him. Over the years spent on land, he had absorbed and contemplated the experience, and then he reached a point where he could recall it and write of the tragedy and darkness. *Heart of Darkness* continues to be one of Conrad's most influential books. He unflinchingly depicts the slavery, the skulls on posts, and the rampant killings. The general public, and even critics, didn't appreciate Conrad's commentary on colonialism and his questioning of "progress." Imperialist ideas were dominant in literature at this point, and *Heart of Darkness* contradicted and questioned these views. Conrad's witnessing of the way Europeans, in the name of civilization, had destroyed and corrupted a land and its peoples, led to his profound understanding and insights into human nature, and the horror of racism and colonialism. Through his writing, Conrad penetrated the human heart and mind. Once Conrad had explored the world as a sailor, now he explored territory as a writer.

During this time he completed the novel *Lord Jim*, which had begun as a short story, then, grew larger, following in the tradition of much of his work. The idea of writing a novel distressed Conrad, so he fell into a pattern of calling the piece a short-story, which then would continue to expand and lengthen into a novel.

The novelist was also noticed and respected in his home country, and his first two novels had been translated into Polish.

Everything Conrad wrote found a publisher, however, he still wanted to increase his income and reach a wider audience. He hoped that by collaborating with Ford, his friend could help him with his English, and also stimulate him to produce his work at a faster pace. While Conrad was working on his own books, the two also worked on their first collaborative novel, *The Inheritors*. The idea of co-writing novels was an established practice during the period. Stevenson and Kipling, for example, had experience with collaborators. This book was Ford's idea, and he did most of the writing; however, they hoped by adding Conrad's name to the piece, they would capture more popularity.

In addition to the stories and novellas he produced, Conrad was still struggling with *The Rescue*. He wrote to Garnett: "The more I write the less substance do I see in my work.... It is tolerably awful. And I face it, I face it but the fight is growing on me." (Watt, 254) He had better success writing one of his longest novels, *Lord Jim*, which he completed just before leaving on holiday. Marguerite Poradowska, whom he had not seen for several years, had invited his family to vacation at a Belgian seaside resort. Ford and his wife also joined them. However, the vacation wasn't pleasant—Conrad's son was ill, and Conrad had trouble working.

Back at Pent Farm, he continued to work on various projects. Then a month before serialization began in *Blackwood's* for the third story of *Youth*, a fire broke out and burned the last half of the manuscript. Ford came to his rescue again. He helped Conrad reconstruct the manuscript, so that he was able to send it off in time to meet the deadline, with Conrad writing through the night until the very last minute.

Even with his various publications and productive writing experience at Pent Farm, Conrad still struggled financially. He continued to borrow money from friends that he couldn't pay back. His debts increased. And although *Blackwood's* paid very well, Conrad worked so slowly that he still could not earn enough for his family to live on. Conrad often asked the publisher for money for stories not yet written, and his stories usually did not arrive by the deadline. Although the publisher and Conrad had developed a working relationship for several years, William Blackwood finally reached the point where he believed Conrad had become unreliable, considering him to be a financial loss to the company, and resulting in Conrad's break with his publisher.

EXHAUSTION AND DISASTERS

At the turn of the 20th century, J.B. Pinker became Conrad's agent. Pinker's clients included Crane, Wells, and Oscar Wilde. When Pinker first approached Conrad in 1899, Conrad truthfully admitted his risk as a client: "My method of writing is so unbusiness-like that I don't think you could have any use for such an unsatisfactory person. I generally sell a work before it is begun, get paid when it is half done and don't do the other half till the spirit moves me." (Meyers, 203) Despite these claims, Pinker took Conrad on. He believed in his writing, and recognized his talents.

However, true to his warning, Conrad was not reliable with finances. Pinker often lent Conrad substantial sums of money, gave him advances, and helped him out of debt. Meyers explains that although Conrad certainly was not making substantial amounts of money, he also didn't reduce his standard of living to match his income, creating years of debt and frustration. (Meyers, 204) Conrad thought he should still be able to have maids, gardeners, tutors, private schools, and vacations, and this way of living only contributed to his financial anxieties.

Conrad's circle of acquaintances continued to grow, as he met Arnold Bennett and Rudyard Kipling. As writers, Kipling and Conrad were rivals, and critics often compared their works, which portrayed imperialism at the height of its dominance. Conrad's relationship with Kipling was complex. The two were friendly with each other, and made visits to each other's homes. However, Conrad resented his work being compared to Kipling's. While he admired Kipling's technical expertise and artistic grace, he thought overall the work was inferior, not profound or ambitious. The most noticeable difference between their work concerned the philosophies behind the novels—while Kipling defended colonialism, Conrad's work challenged, even overturned, these ideas.

For two years Conrad dedicated his time to the novel *Nostromo*, a novel perhaps initially inspired by Cunninghame Graham and his experiences of South America. Conrad had also sailed to South America on one of his earliest sailing trips, but spent only a brief time there. Whereas everything up to this point had been based mostly on personal experience, this novel was grounded very much in imagination. This novel, like much of his other work, questions colonialism and "progress."

Writing this complex, ambitious novel consumed and exhausted Conrad. He struggled with his own deteriorating health, fighting several attacks of gout. Then in 1904, walking out of a department store, Jessie had a terrible fall, badly injuring her knees, which would semi-cripple her for the rest of her life. Money problems continued to escalate, with bills, repayment of loans, and now doctor bills for Jessie's surgery. Conrad's bankers, Watson & Co., failed, worsening the financial difficulties. Conrad, nerve-wracked and exhausted, needed a holiday to recuperate.

After Jessie's first surgery and Conrad's completion of *Nostromo*, they vacationed in Capri for four months, with hopes that the mild Mediterranean climate would help with Jessie's recovery, and provide rest for Conrad. Conrad had hoped not only to relax, but also to write; however, the trip, like many of their vacations, was a disaster. Jessie had to be swung in a chair on to ships and trains because of her knees, and several accidents nearly occurred. For example, in Rome where they were changing trains, the porters removed Jessie's chair too soon and left her hanging from the side of the railway car. Conrad, terrified, nearly fainted at the sight. Then, in Capri, Jessie's nurse became ill, and Conrad soon followed, suffering from influenza, bronchitis, and a terrible toothache. Instead of helping his nerves, the trip only intensified his anxiety, and he felt relieved to return home.

On their return to England, Conrad was involved in the production of his one-act play, *One Day More,* and in addition to his fiction, he worked on autobiographical sea sketches for *Mirror of the Sea,* much of which he dictated to Ford. For a short time the Conrads rented rooms to be closer to Ford, so that Conrad and Ford could work together.

His challenging novel *Nostromo,* which he had mentally and physically exhausted himself for, did not sell to the general public, and critics gave disappointing reviews. Conrad was displeased and frustrated by this response, referring to the novel and its reception as "the blackest possible frost." (Sherry, 87) Jessie claimed this was his biggest literary disappointment.

After their son had been quite ill with scarlet fever, the Conrads again left England to recuperate, this time in Montpellier, near the south coast of France. When he returned to England, he collaborated with Ford on a novella. Then on August 2, 1906, the Conrads' second son, John, was born.

The entire family went on yet another disastrous trip, this time to Montpellier and Geneva. Here, the oldest son, Borys, fell ill, catching measles, bronchitis, and rheumatic fever. While Conrad revised *The Secret Agent,* a psychological and detective novel dealing with anarchists, Jessie cared for Borys, and Conrad admitted, "Jessie has been simply heroic." (Sherry, 90) The Conrads then stayed in Champel for convalescence. Conrad stated, "No more trips abroad. I am sick of them." (Meyers, 233) If anything good came out of the trip, it was that Borys's illness and slow recovery affected Conrad's relationship with his son, and he became closer to him, often reading books aloud to him.

When the Conrads returned to England, doctors advised them to leave Pent Farm because of the dampness in Kent, which seemed to be affecting the health of the entire family. So they moved to a farm house, Someries, in Bedfordshire, a roomy place much bigger than Pent Farm.

BREAK DOWN

At fifty, Conrad had reached great acclaim over the years, but he still felt anxious and disappointed that he was not a more popular and successful author. With his foreboding outlook on humanity and industrial progress, his work seemed to be too dark for both critics and the public. Conrad felt caught between needing to make money, and wanting to maintain his artistic integrity. He wrote Galsworthy, "You don't know what an inspiration-killing anxiety it is to think: 'Is it saleable?' There's nothing more cruel than to be caught between one's impulse, one's act, and that question, which for me is simply a question of life and death."(Sherry, 94) This question wouldn't go away. A year later, in a letter to a friend, he railed against the more popular authors: "They are popular because they express the common thought, and the common man is delighted to find himself in accord with people he supposes distinguished." (Sherry, 94) Conrad's philosophies and complex questions about the nature of humans were integral to his work, so that he felt he could not write a novel with mass appeal.

Conrad had begun his novel, *Under Western Eyes*, and during the creation, he again suffered from gout and worried about money problems, his debt had accumulated even more. In addition to these troubles, Jessie had several unsuccessful operations on her knees. The fall had left her a semi-invalid, and she had to endure intense pain.

Someries proved too noisy for Conrad to work, and so the family moved again. Now the Conrads were living back in Kent, this time in a small apartment above a butcher's shop in the village of Aldington, in which Conrad's study was no bigger than a cubicle, without windows. This place was noisy, and the smells from the butcher shop rose up into their home. The squalor setting added to Conrad's feelings of depression and failure.

However, he continued to work on his novel. During this time, he had an unexpected visitor, a sea captain who wanted to let Conrad know how much he appreciated his writing. Conrad felt grateful and quite moved by the sailor's admiration. This visit also returned him to his memories, those long-past sea-faring days. He told Pinker, "I had a visit from a man out of the Malay Seas. It was like the raising of a lot of dead—dead to me, because most of them live out there and even read my books and wonder who the devil has been around taking notes...."

(Meyers, 263) This visit inspired several short stories, and also carried Conrad back to his past, remembering both the adventure and also the hardships of sailing life.

In his present life, not as a sailor but as a writer, creativity, money, and friendships felt as if they were crumbling before his eyes. After spending many years collaborating on fiction, and also developing a close friendship, Conrad and Ford's relationship began to unravel. Ford had started the *English Review*, a prestigious journal publishing D.H. Lawrence and Ezra Pound, and his new success and power affected their friendship. Part of their quarrel rose from the fact that Conrad had failed to submit a chapter of *A Personal Record* to Ford's new, highly-esteemed journal by the deadline. But the argument was also more complex, with Conrad now distancing himself from Ford, bothered by Ford's "megalomania." (Meyers, 248) The quarrel led to a distanced, estranged relationship.

In addition to the falling out with Ford, Conrad also had a major quarrel with his agent, Pinker. *Under Western Eyes* had absorbed Conrad, and the novel proceeded to grow and mushroom. He continued to tell Pinker the novel would be finished soon, yet in reality, the end seemed very far off. When Pinker refused to advance any more funds, Conrad reacted furiously, threatening to throw the manuscript into the fire. He wrote an angry letter to Galsworthy complaining about Pinker: "Does he think I am the sort of man who wouldn't finish the story in a week if he could? ... I sit twelve hours at the table, sleep six, and worry the rest of the time, feeling the age creeping on and looking at those I love. For two years I haven't seen a picture, heard a note of music, hadn't a moment of ease in human intercourse—not really. And he talks of *regular supplies of manuscript.*" (Meyers, 252) Then six months later, after completing the novel, Conrad went to Pinker's office in London. In reaction to Pinker's threats and refusals to advance funds, Conrad got into a heated argument with him. This severe quarrel led to a two-year estrangement.

Returning to Aldington, after the quarrel with Pinker, the build-up of these conflicts had reached its climax—Conrad had a nervous breakdown. The mental effects were accompanied by physical symptoms, such as a feverish delirium. For two years Conrad had been working nonstop on *Under Western Eyes*, while suffering from attacks of gout. His work always exhausted him, as he completely immersed himself in the fictional worlds he created.

Under Western Eyes takes place in Switzerland and Russia, and some
of the descriptions probably came from his experience there as a child:

> "Under the sumptuous immensity of the sky, the snow
> covered endless forests, the frozen rivers, the plains of an
> immense country, obliterating the landmarks, the accidents
> of the ground, leveling everything under its uniform
> whiteness, like a monstrous black page awaiting the record of
> an inconceivable history."

Conrad still felt deep resentment toward Russia, and writing this
consuming novel affected him emotionally even more so than his other
works so far. He recalled the environment as being bleak and vast. What
he remembered about Russia was that it was a place where he was treated
like a criminal, that forbade the use of his native tongue, and led to, if
not caused, the deaths of his parents. Many critics believe this book to
be the last of Conrad's that truly examined human nature, the universe,
and the fate of humankind; this work did not lend itself to popularity,
and also emotionally and psychologically drained Conrad.

The strains with money, health, and creative anxiety proved to be
too overwhelming, and now the estrangement with Ford and Pinker had
pushed him over the edge. Jessie explained, "The novel is finished, but
the penalty has to be paid. Months of nervous strain have ended in a
complete nervous breakdown. Poor Conrad is very ill and Dr Hackney
says it will be a long time before he is fit for anything requiring mental
exertion." (Sherry, 95) Conrad had always been high-strung, pessimistic,
and deeply absorbed in his work, and the culmination of these
characteristics with his constant financial and health problems,
eventually led to this nervous breakdown.

RECOVERY, POPULARITY, AND WAR

Conrad spent several months recovering from his nervous breakdown. A
change in environment seemed crucial, and so the Conrads moved out
of their home above the butcher shop. Conrad felt more content when
they moved to Capel House, an isolated farmhouse near Ashford.
Although the house lacked electricity and hot water, the seventeenth
century home was quite spacious, with a garden and attractive landscape,

and a warm, cozy atmosphere. Woods, ponds, and an orchard of fruit trees made up the land. During this recovery period, Conrad spent the days being fairly isolated. Although he still wrote letters to his friends, as usual lavishing them with encouragement about their own work, while hesitating with his own, he did not socialize in person as often.

However, Conrad was on the road to recovery, and also, to fame. He was awarded a Civil List pension, which helped out a little with his finances. He had also returned to a novel he had started several years ago, then abandoned, and he wrote the entire book quite easily between the summer of 1911 and spring of 1912. *Chance* was serialized by the *New York Herald.* A young employee of Doubleday, Alfred Knopf, persuaded his employers to put their full weight and support behind the book. The book was marked with an attractive cover, with the picture of a woman, and catchy chapter titles to help sales. Consequently, Conrad's reputation grew in England and America. For the first time, Conrad had written a bestseller on both sides of the Atlantic. With the success of *Chance*, he reached the fame for which he'd been waiting for fifteen years; he had finally reached the masses, without feeling as if he'd lost his artistic integrity.

As he became more celebrated, Conrad's circles of literary friends continued to grow and flourish. At this time, he met Richard Curle, a young aristocrat, and great admirer of Conrad's work. Curle had written a published critical appreciation of Conrad, and was later to write many articles and several books about him, helping to sustain Conrad's reputation. After their first meeting, the two began to form a close friendship, and Conrad treated the much younger man as if he were a son. He also met Andre Gide, who translated many of his works into French.

Strengthened by his new success, and now more financially secure with the money from his book, Conrad decided to visit Poland with his family. He felt rejuvenated for a change of scenery and a chance to travel. Conrad hadn't been in Poland since before Tadeusz died; it was an absence of twenty-one years. Understandably, he was eager to show his family his roots, and also to revisit his homeland as a successful author. So he continued on with the trip, despite portentous signs of war.

On the first day in Cracow, where he had spent time growing up, he took Borys with him to visit the Jagiellonian Library. The librarian then showed Conrad his father's letters and manuscripts, and Conrad was quite moved. He had always assumed that his father's writings had been lost or destroyed. Instead, Apollo's works had been collected and preserved. Conrad felt reminiscent and touched. He continued to revisit the sites of his childhood with nostalgia, pointing out the places to his family.

However, the sentimental mood ended in immediate danger. While the Conrads were in Cracow, Austria-Hungary declared war on Serbia in July, and on August 1, Germany declared war on Russia and then invaded France. World War I had started. Fearful of imprisonment or being caught in battle, Conrad took his family to stay with a distant relative in Zakopane, a resort in the Tatra Mountains. They were unable to leave, and had no choice but to stay on with the relatives. During this time, Conrad read some Polish literature, but spent most of his energy reading the news and analyzing the political climate. Then, through connections of friends, the Conrads were finally able to travel to Vienna, after spending two months in Zakopane. After five days in Vienna, they went on to then still-neutral Italy, and then they safely reached England.

World War I had started, and, the war years were grim for Conrad—as they were for most people in Europe—despite his new success. His next novel, *Victory*, was even more successful than *Chance*. However, Conrad had other matters on his mind. His son, Borys, joined the army, and Conrad worried about his survival. With the exception of letters, he wrote very little during these years. He had always been an avid letter writer, and now he wrote many letters to his son, able to connect with him more by written words than verbal.

Although anxious, Conrad was not inactive or antisocial during this time. He continued to meet new people, and broaden his already wide circle of friends. In 1916 he met the American bohemian, Jane Anderson, and for a short time the two were quite close. Conrad became enamored of her reckless, adventure-seeking personality; scholars have debated whether he had an affair with Jane. Conrad would have been the last one to admit such personal information. He was very careful in all of his autobiographical work to never embarrass himself or others, and he had a strong sense of what he deemed society thought acceptable or not. Although tolerant of the affairs and sexual tastes of his friends (Galsworthy, Garnett, Ford, Wells all had affairs, Crane's wife was a former prostitute, and Casement, Gide, and Norman Douglas were gay), he did not "approve." So if he indeed had an affair, he would have been extremely secretive about it. Even if they did not have an affair, scholars agree that Conrad and Jane's relationship affected Jessie, causing arguments and jealousy in the household.

Perhaps inspired by Jane's dangerous life (at one point she was a war correspondent), Conrad also wanted to contribute something to the war. During this time, he felt quite patriotic as a British citizen. He visited several ports to get an idea of the naval activities, and he was treated very well by the sailors—he enjoyed the camaraderie. He was offered a chance to go to sea with them for a short trip, and so he became involved in a plan to observe activities in various British ports. He set out on a twelve-day cruise on a boat disguised as a merchant vessel, in the hopes of luring German submarines into a deadly trap. The trip, however, was uneventful, except for the bad weather. His short involvement in the military was stimulating and adventurous, but his poor health sent him back to his family and his desk.

Then, Conrad's fear about his son came true—Borys was gassed and shell-shocked in combat. Conrad felt even more that the future of humanity was hopeless. Furthermore, at home, Jessie's problems with her knee worsened, and she required another series of operations, which were all unsuccessful, leaving her in great pain, and without mobility. Conrad worried extensively over both his wife and son, and also struggled with his own physical ailments. By the end of the war, his pessimistic outlook prevailed, and he saw no real hope for the future. His negative feelings toward Russia, which had started as a young child when his family was sent into exile, always stayed with him. He was bewildered that the Bolsheviks were invited to the Peace Conference. Even when Poland was finally freed after 123 years of oppression and recognized as an independent state, Conrad did not have high expectations. The war had only solidified his despairing feelings and his dark views.

AFTER THE WAR

In the years after the war, Conrad was experiencing a tremendous amount of physical and emotional weariness. However, he wrote literary and political essays, and worked on his fiction. For pleasure, Conrad listened to music, mostly opera. He also continued to sell his manuscripts, and took an interest in his works being translated. Remarkably, after not touching the manuscript that had caused him so much anxiety and trouble for twenty years, Conrad now returned to *The Rescue.* This time he finished the book without trouble. He simply picked up where he left off twenty years ago, and completed the story. Frank Doubleday recalled, "Nobody can tell where the old part ended and the new began." (Meyers, 336)

In the fall of 1919, after their landlord died, the Conrads moved to Oswalds, a home near Canterbury. The Conrads had never owned a home, always paying rent, and Capel had been the place where they lived for nearly a decade. Their new home was spacious and elegant, and almost a century old. Trees surrounded the house, and ivy grew on the walls. This rented home, unlike so many of the others, was equipped with electricity and heating. Conrad hired servant help, including a butler, maid, and cook. The Conrads now had more money and less accumulated debt. Conrad's reputation continued to grow, with critical studies on his work being published, and he received substantial money from a collected edition of his work and also from his work being sold for film rights. He received a $12,000 advance on an American collected edition, and 10,000 pounds on an English collected edition. He also sold many of his manuscripts to a wealthy American lawyer, John Quinn. However, not surprisingly, Conrad still found it difficult not to overspend: "I am spending more than I ought to—and I am constitutionally unable to put on the brake unless in such a manner as to smash everything." (Sherry, 107) He liked living an aristocratic life, and could not make the adjustments in his lifestyle to match his income. He also wanted more prestige, and hoped for the Nobel prize.

Conrad worked on the dramatization of *The Secret Agent,* and a dramatization of *Victory* was performed at the Globe Theater in London. In 1921, Conrad and Jessie and her nurse traveled to Corsica, the French island where Napoleon was born. Conrad had an interest in Napoleon, and while he was there he researched and read about Napoleon for a novel he had in mind. His paternal grandfather had been a lieutenant in Napoleon's army, and once the Poles had placed their hope in Napoleon bringing them independence and freedom. However, in his autobiographical writings, Conrad distanced himself from this history, expressing distaste for Napoleon's methods. He also started another novel, called *The Rover.* However, for the most part, this trip resembled so many of the vacations taken in their earlier days: Conrad was restless and unable to work. He protested that he couldn't sum up the creative energy, yet despite these complaints, he spent time significant time writing.

A year later, Conrad lost a good friend. J.B. Pinker, ill with the flu, died at age fifty-eight. Conrad had more than a business relationship with Pinker—he considered him an invaluable friend. He felt very close to Pinker, despite their earlier falling out, and his death came as a terrible shock.

Conrad was now one of the most famous living authors in England and America, and finally, he was more financially secure. In the spring of 1923 he made his only visit to America. He had declined on a earlier invite, but now, post-war, he accepted the invitation from his publisher Frank Doubleday. Conrad traveled by a steamship, as a passenger, of course, and the journey did not at all resemble his youthful days of sailing. The danger and excitement he'd seen in his days had been replaced by technology, and the giant ship seemed dull and too safe, without any of the romantic qualities of an old sailing ship.

Conrad's hope was to keep the trip to America low-key and to avoid publicity; however, as soon as the ship landed, a mass of journalists and cameras awaited him. Also, a crowd of Poles greeted him with flowers. Conrad felt ill, exhausted and weak, and Doubleday tried to whisk him away from the mob. He stayed sheltered at Doubleday's estate in Oyster Bay, Long Island, but he couldn't stay completely isolated. He gave a few interviews, and then presented an informal lecture and reading at the home of Mrs. Curtis James, a wealthy socialite living on Park Avenue. Doubleday described Conrad as "in a state of nervous collapse ... [The public talk] nearly killed him, because of his extreme nervousness."(Meyers, 351) Reactions to the reading differed, from people expressing boredom to interest, although most accounts showed Conrad's talk went on for over two hours, and that he spoken in very broken English, in a nervous tone of voice. Conrad, however, described the event as being well received, in which he moved his audience to laughter and tears.

He spent a month in America, staying under the care of the Doubledays, even going on a ten-day trip through New England with them. When he returned to England, he found out that Borys had concealed something from him—his marriage. Conrad's temper flared when Jessie told him the news; he was angry that this event had been kept a secret from him.

After his trip to America, Conrad battled illness and worked on *Suspense*, the Napoleonic novel, which was his last (and unfinished) book. He was also sitting for the artist Jacob Epstein who sculpted a bust of his likeness. Epstein observed, "He was crippled with rheumatism, crotchety, nervous, and ill." (Sherry, 113)

During this last period of his life, Conrad was offered a knighthood. An envelope that he assumed was an income tax statement sat unopened on his desk, and after some time had passed, a personal messenger from the Prime Minister arrived at his door. Embarrassed, Conrad realized what actually was inside the unopened envelope—a letter offering him knighthood. Although honored, Conrad declined, feeling that it was inappropriate for an artist to accept that sort of privilege.

He suffered a heart attack in July of 1924, and he continued to be quite weak and ill. He also struggled with depression. His long-time friend and supporter Edward Garnett recalled the last time he saw Conrad, that "something moved me as we said good night, to put his hand to my lips. He then embraced me with a long and silent pressure." (Sherry, 114) Conrad survived another heart attack two months after the first.

The morning after this second heart attack, he called to Jessie to tell her he was feeling better. Then at 8:30 he slid from his chair to the floor. He died at the age of sixty-six on August 3, 1924.

WORKS CITED

Conrad, Joseph. *The Mirror of the Sea & A Personal Record*. Oxford: Oxford University Press, 1988.

Gillon, Adam. *Joseph Conrad*. Boston: Twayne Publishers, 1982.

Jean-Aubry, Gerard. *The Sea Dreamer: A Definitive Biography of Joseph Conrad*. New York: Archon Books, 1967.

Karl, Frederick R. and Laurence Davies, eds. *The Collected Letters of Joseph Conrad, volume 1, 1861-1897*. Cambridge: Cambridge University Press, 62.

Meyers, Jeffrey. *Joseph Conrad: A Biography*. New York: Charles Scribner's Sons, 1991.

Najder, Zdzislaw. *Joseph Conrad: A Chronicle*. New Brunswick: Rutgers University Press, 1983.

Sherry, Norman. *Conrad*. New York: Thames & Hudson, 1972.

Watt, Ian. *Conrad in the Nineteenth Century*. Berkeley: University of California Press, 1979.

RICHARD RUPPEL

Introduction to the Works
of Joseph Conrad

ART INTO LIFE: LIFE INTO ART

Early in the year 1878, Joseph Conrad (who still went by his given name, Józef Teodor Konrad Korzeniowski) had just turned 20 and, following the practice of many people that age, looked closely into the direction of his life. He came to a despairing conclusion. He was in debt; he may have been disappointed in love, and his career prospects were unpromising. So he wrote a long note to a good friend, invited him over, and shot himself in the chest.

Those familiar with Conrad up to that point would have been unsurprised, for his life had been very difficult. Born a Pole, his country existed as a culture and a language, but not as a nation. Austria, Russia, and Prussia had partitioned Poland at the end of the 18th century, and, despite repeated, heroic insurrections throughout the 19th century, Poland did not regain its independence until 1918. Conrad's father and mother, Apollo Korzeniowski and Ewelina Bobrowska Korzeniowski, were both Polish patriots. When Conrad was four, the Korzeniowskis were convicted of treason against Russia and were exiled to Vologda, a penal colony in Northern Russia. The conditions were unhealthy—long, terrible winters and short, wet summers. Ewa died of tuberculosis when Conrad was seven, and Apollo died of the same illness when he was eleven. Conrad led thousands of mourners during Apollo's funeral procession in 1869.

Following their deaths, Conrad was raised by his mother's brother, Tadeusz Bobrowski. Bobrowski had little respect for Conrad's father. He insisted that Apollo had acted irresponsibly and quixotically, that his revolutionary activities had led to the death of Ewa and the destruction of his family. As long as Bobrowski was alive, he warned Conrad not to follow in Apollo's "romantic" footsteps.[1]

Conrad left Poland when he was sixteen; he had decided to become a sailor, and Poland had no seaports. But another reason must have been that he felt he had no future in his native country. His father and mother had left him a noble legacy of principled resistance to oppression. At the same time, his pragmatic uncle insisted that he reject that legacy, compromise with the colonial occupiers who had killed his parents, and seek to achieve financial success. Conrad was a proud, fiery young man, a *szlachcic*, or member of the Polish nobility, and he could never chart a middle course between these two irreconcilable choices; he saw the futility of revolutionary action, but he scorned political compromise and the pursuit of money for its own sake. So he fled land-locked Poland to go to sea, and he joined the expatriate Polish community in Marseilles.

He had a substantial allowance from his uncle, and he had access to his inheritance from Apollo, so he lived well in Marseilles and began to learn the arts of seamanship. But he was a very young man in a world full of temptations, and he lavished gifts on his acquaintances, gambled, and went into debt. When he invited his friend, Richard Fecht, to his apartment for tea, he must have been hopeless. He owed Fecht 800 francs: at that time, a very large sum of money. He wrote out the names and addresses of his friends, leveled a revolver at his chest, and pulled the trigger just before Fecht's arrival. Here is how his uncle described the experience:

> Suddenly ... I received a telegram: 'Conrad blessé envoyez argent—arrivez' [Conrad has been wounded—send money and come yourself] ... [Conrad,] wishing to improve his finances, tries his luck in Monte Carlo and loses the 800 fr. he had borrowed. Having managed his affairs so excellently he returns to Marseilles and one fine evening invites his friend the creditor to tea, and before his arrival attempts to take his life with a revolver. (Let this detail remain between us, as I have been telling everyone that he was wounded in a

duel....)   The bullet goes durch und durch [through and through] near his heart without damaging any vital organ. Luckily, all his addresses were left on top of his things so that this worthy Mr Fecht could instantly let me know... [2]

Conrad recovered quickly from the wound—he was walking by the time Bobrowski arrived ten days later. His uncle paid his debts, and that same year Conrad left for England to join the British merchant marines.

Though his English was imperfect, and though he had no connections at all in England, Conrad rose rapidly, beginning as an "Ordinary Seaman." He passed his "Second Mate" certificate in 1880, his "First Mate" certificate (after one failure) in 1884, and his "Master" certificate (again after one failure) in 1886, meanwhile becoming a naturalized English citizen.[3] This is an astonishing accomplishment in so short a time period.

Conrad remained at sea for the next eight years, and his experiences supplied most of the material that he later worked into his fiction. His voyages took him to the Malay archipelago, to Australia, and up the Congo River into what was then the Belgian Congo. This last was an ill-fated trip. In 1890, Conrad was offered command of a steam ship for a Belgian company. (Belgium had become the colonial power in the Congo in 1885.) Steam ships were used to move supplies and cargo— primarily ivory and rubber—up and down the Congo River. Conrad felt that he was mistreated by the Belgians who controlled the company. More significantly, he became very ill with dysentery and fever. Though he had signed a three-year contract, he was discharged for health reasons; he had spent a total of six months in Africa. He recovered enough to remain a seaman for three more years, but he never fully recovered his health, and this must have contributed to his decision in 1894 to leave the sea for good and to become a writer.

Conrad's lifelong habit of fictionalizing his life—critics didn't discover that the "dueling" injury was a suicide attempt, for example, until long after Conrad's death in 1924—is the corollary to his creative technique of turning his life into fiction. Researchers have found real-life counterparts for nearly all of his characters, and the most significant incidents in his greatest works are based on Conrad's experiences, travel literature, or newspaper accounts. Strictly speaking, he doesn't seem to have "invented" very many incidents or characters. The setting, characters, and incidents in his two African stories, "An Outpost of Progress" and *Heart of Darkness*, derived from his time in Africa. *Heart of Darkness*, in fact, is a barely fictionalized autobiography, augmented by his reading of other traveler's accounts. The stealing of a fortune in silver from a lighter (a large boat used to haul cargo), the central incident in *Nostromo*, originated from a newspaper story about an Italian sailor who managed to accomplish this in South America.

TALES OF ADVENTURE

Conrad was a self-conscious artist, a proud craftsman who scorned the popular adventure fiction of his day—the works of authors such as Rider Haggard and John Buchan. But he wrote adventure fiction which was set, for the most part, in exotic locations, so his work put him in direct competition with Haggard, Rudyard Kipling, Robert Louis Stevenson, and other popular authors at the end of the nineteenth century. This often produces a tension in his novels between the conventions of adventure fiction—where authors might introduce "exotic" elements for their own sake, and where they might treat these elements in stereotypical ways—and the demands of both truth and the art that Conrad valued so highly.

There are scenes in some of Conrad's greatest work that might have been written by far less ambitious and accomplished authors. Here is an example—a brief episode from *Nostromo* involving the novel's adventure hero (an Italian sailor nicknamed Nostromo and the "Capatez de Cargadores," "chief of the waterfront") in a dispute with his (temporary) girlfriend:

> Her arms and neck emerged plump and bare from a snowy chemisette; the blue woollen skirt, with all the fullness gathered in front, scanty on the hips and tight across the back, disclosed the provoking action of her walk. She came straight on and laid her hand on the mare's neck with a timid, coquettish look upwards out of the corner of her eyes.
>
> "Querido [Darling]," she murmured, caressingly, "why do you pretend not to see me when I pass?"
>
> "Because I don't love thee any more," said Nostromo, deliberately, after a moment of reflective silence.

The hand on the mare's neck trembled suddenly. She dropped her head before all the eyes in the wide circle formed round the generous, the terrible, the inconstant Capataz de Cargadores, and his Morenita.

Nostromo, looking down, saw tears beginning to fall down her face.

"Has it come, then, ever beloved of my heart?" she whispered. "Is it true?"

"No," said Nostromo, looking away carelessly. "It was a lie. I love thee as much as ever."

"Is that true?" she cooed, joyously, her cheeks still wet with tears.

"It is true." (127-28)[4]

But she is angered when Nostromo refuses to give her any money:

"Juan," she hissed, "I could stab thee to the heart!"

The dreaded Capataz de Cargadores, magnificent and carelessly public in his amours, flung his arm round her neck and kissed her spluttering lips. A murmur went round.

"A knife!" he demanded at large, holding her firmly by the shoulder.

Twenty blades flashed out together in the circle. A young man in holiday attire, bounding in, thrust one in Nostromo's hand and bounded back into the ranks, very proud of himself. Nostromo had not even looked at him.

"Stand on my foot," he commanded the girl, who, suddenly subdued, rose lightly, and when he had her up, encircling her waist, her face near to his, he pressed the knife into her little hand.

"No, Morenita! You shall not put me to shame," he said. "You shall have your present; and so that everyone should know who is your lover to-day, you may cut all the silver buttons off my coat."

There were shouts of laughter and applause at this witty freak, while the girl passed the keen blade, and the impassive rider jingled in his palm the increasing hoard of silver buttons. He eased her to the ground with both her hands full. After whispering for a while with a very strenuous face,

she walked away, staring haughtily, and vanished into the
crowd. (129-30)

Though we might enjoy this scene between Nostromo and his
"Morenita" (which means "little dark girl"), it could easily have been
lifted from a good deal of the popular exotic fiction of Conrad's day. The
end of the novel has been criticized for having something of the same
qualities.

Conrad's work in the exotic, adventure genre has left him open to
a more serious criticism; his representation of non-whites has been
called racist. In the most famous attack ever leveled against Conrad's
work, Chinua Achebe, a great Nigerian novelist who wrote *Things Fall
Apart*, called him a "thoroughgoing racist" for his representation of
Africans in *Heart of Darkness*, which he characterized as "an offensive and
deplorable book."[5] As a number of critics have demonstrated, however,
Achebe overstates his case. Some of his charges can be answered fairly
simply. Conrad, like other Europeans, had little direct knowledge of
Africans, and he was limited in his ability to represent them accurately.
(Achebe accuses him of making his Africans subhuman by denying them
speech, for example, but it's more likely that Conrad gave them little
speech simply because he, and his fictional counterpart, Marlow, could
not understand their language.) And Conrad's attack through *Heart of
Darkness* on the brutal exploitation of Africans by the Europeans was
unprecedented. But Conrad's genre—adventure fiction set in the
colonial world, with its conventional, stereotypical representations of
non-white peoples and exotic settings—was racist almost by definition,
and Achebe raised a number of issues that continue to be debated among
Conrad readers.

There is, finally, some irony in this debate. One reason that
Conrad had difficulty competing with more popular writers of exotic
fiction was that he never celebrated the British Empire and European
imperialism in a straightforward way. All of his fiction criticizes—
sometimes subtly, sometimes directly—the oppression of one people by
another. But his criticism, along with his dark themes and stylistic
innovations, prevented him from becoming a more popular writer, and
he had written all of his most important fiction before he became
anything like a popular success (with the publication, in 1913, of *Chance*).
During his lifetime, in other words, he was unpopular in part because he

criticized imperialism and the Europeans' belief in their racial superiority. Now he is criticized by some readers for not criticizing imperialism and racism more forcefully.

CONRAD'S AESTHETICS: DELAYED DECODING

Throughout his career, Conrad was concerned with epistemology—with how we know what we know. Impressionism is usually associated with late-nineteenth century French painters, but critics also apply the label to some novelists. For Conrad, impressionism refers to his attempt to recreate the way we experience and come to understand an event. Though he himself rejected the title of "impressionist," Conrad was identified as one of its chief practitioners just after his death by Ford Madox Ford (another fine novelist, and a close friend and collaborator with Conrad through the most creative portion of Conrad's writing career). Joseph Warren Beach confirmed the identification in 1932, and this definition of his style was accepted by most critics.[6] Ian Watt refined the concept by inventing the phrase "delayed decoding," a subset of impressionism that very neatly characterizes some of Conrad's most intense passages—such as Marlow's descriptions of the Grove of Death and the attack on the steamer in *Heart of Darkness*.[7] Here is the way Conrad has his narrator, Marlow, describe an attack on the steam ship that Marlow is piloting up the Congo River in order to bring supplies to Kurtz, the European trader who has gone mad in the jungle:

> I was looking down at the sounding-pole, and feeling much annoyed to see at each try a little more of it stick out of that river, when I saw my poleman give up on the business suddenly, and stretch himself flat on the deck, without even taking the trouble to haul his pole in. He kept hold on it though, and it trailed in the water. At the same time the fireman, whom I could also see below me, sat down abruptly before his furnace and ducked his head. I was amazed. Then I had to look at the river mighty quick, because there was a snag in the fairway. Sticks, little sticks, were flying about, thick; they were whizzing before my nose, dropping below me, striking behind me against my pilot-house. All this time the river, the shore, the woods, were very quiet—perfectly

quiet. I could only hear the heavy splashing thump of the
stern-wheel and the patter of these things. We cleared the
snag clumsily. Arrows, by Jove! We were being shot at![8]

In this remarkable description of the attack, Conrad has recreated how
we receive and process information. Captain Marlow is preoccupied
with nursing a clumsy ship up a narrow river. He worries about snags
and sandbars that might damage the hull; he worries about the leaking,
unreliable steam engine; he worries about the reliability of his crew, and
he especially worries that he'll run his ship aground. These
preoccupations prevent him from being able to process new information
quickly. So he's simply amazed that his crew has stopped working. How
can they stop? The ship will run aground! Then he notices little
"sticks" flying through the air and striking the ship. And now he finally
understands: "Arrows, by Jove! We were being shot at!"

Conrad made use of this technique in many different
circumstances. In *Nostromo*, both the characters and the reader get their
information piecemeal, in many different ways: from characters (who
might be unreliable or simply wrong), from letters, from incomplete
conversations, and from the omniscient narrative itself.

THE UNRELIABLE NARRATOR

Another of Conrad's innovations is the unreliable narrator. Conrad did
not invent this technique, certainly (the narrator of the *Canterbury Tales*,
named "Chaucer," can't always be equated with the author), but he
carried the implications of the narrator's lack of reliability further than
anyone else, and he used the technique with great subtlety. Captain
Marlow in *Heart of Darkness*, *Lord Jim*, "Youth," and *Chance* is often
associated with Conrad himself. Like Conrad, he is a seaman, and many
of his experiences are recreations of Conrad's experiences. But, unlike
Conrad, he is an Englishman, with English prejudices. (He doesn't much
like the French, though there's no evidence that Conrad disliked
France—his first choice of exile, and the land of his second language.)
And we can't always trust his judgments when his sympathies are
engaged. He takes a profound liking for the eponymous protagonist in
Lord Jim, for example, though Jim committed the most unforgivable
crime of a naval officer—he deserted his passengers and was one of the

first to abandon a sinking ship. Despite this, Marlow works very hard to support and encourage Jim. It's unlikely that Captain Conrad would have supported a sailor guilty of such a terrible dereliction of duty. The narrator of *Under Western Eyes* and various speakers in *Nostromo* are all unreliable in subtle and revealing ways.

CENTRAL THEMES: FIDELITY & IDENTITY IN *LORD JIM* AND *UNDER WESTERN EYES*

One way to explore Conrad's themes is to examine how he deals with antithetical concepts: fidelity vs. betrayal, fixed vs. uncertain personal identity, social justice vs. the certainty that all social institutions are imperfect. The fidelity of nearly all of Conrad's protagonists is tested, and very often they fail. We seldom entirely blame them, however, for Conrad's world is full of impossible choices. They are often left, as Marlow says in *Heart of Darkness*, with "a choice of nightmares."[9] So, in *Heart of Darkness*, Marlow must choose between the venal traders and the insane, even murderous Kurtz. In *Lord Jim*, Jim must choose between heroic duty and self-preservation, and later between fidelity to an ideal of honor and fidelity to the woman he loves. Nostromo must choose among loyalty to his own people—the working poor of Sulaco—loyalty to his masters, or loyalty to himself. Once these protagonists make these choices, they betray someone's trust.

The problem of identity is a related theme. The famous Stein, a German trader, entomologist, and philosopher in *Lord Jim*, articulates this problem as well as anyone, despite his broken English:

> "We want in so many different ways to be," he began again. "This magnificent butterfly finds a little heap of dirt and sits still on it; but man he will never on his heap of mud keep still. He want to be so, and again he want to be so...." He moved his hand up, then down.... "He wants to be a saint, and he wants to be a devil—and every time he shuts his eyes he sees himself as a very fine fellow—so fine as he can never be ..."[10]

Few important characters in Conrad's works are happy with their identities. At best, they learn to accept compromises, to live their failings. At worst, they despair, betray themselves and their own ideals, or even commit suicide.

One such tormented figure is Razumov of *Under Western Eyes* (1911), a novel that deals with issues of identity, betrayal, and the crushing effectiveness of despotism—represented by the government of Tsar Nicholas II of Russia. Razumov is a promising university student, the illegitimate son of a Russian nobleman. He is drawn, unwittingly, into the plans of a radical group, betrays its young leader, and becomes a secret agent for the Russian government. Caught between a heartless, despotic government and the equally heartless, radical groups that grow up to oppose it, Razumov's tragic isolation anticipates the situations of characters in the works of Kafka, Becket, and post-modern authors such as Harold Pinter and Kazuo Ishiguro. In some ways, *Under Western Eyes* is unlike anything else Conrad wrote. Based in St. Petersburg and Geneva, it is the only Conrad novel set on the European continent, and all of its important characters, with the exception of the unnamed narrator, are Russians. It is also his most explicitly political novel.

But it addresses many of his great themes: the search for identity, the effect of social forces on the individual, the (often destructive) role of ideas in people's lives, and the difficulty of achieving intimacy between men and between men and women—all told by a well-meaning but limited and unreliable narrator.

SOCIAL JUSTICE & INJUSTICE: *THE SECRET AGENT*

In *The Secret Agent: A Simple Tale* (1907), social justice and injustice are two of Conrad's central concerns. Conrad creates a dark image of late 19th century London, where the glitter of the rich deepens the gloom in poor neighborhoods. In a harrowing scene, the secret agent's mother-in-law takes a cab to a bare, retirement flat, driven by a miserable cabby behind a crippled horse. Only Stevie, her mentally handicapped son, can appreciate the pathos of the scene and provide a moral commentary, but his vocabulary is woefully inadequate. When his sister, Winnie, calls the horse a "Poor brute," Stevie cries: "Poor! Poor!" in agreement. Then he adds, "Cabman poor, too. He told me himself." "Poor brute, poor people!" "Shame!" And finally he articulates the complete, revolutionary thought: "Bad world for poor people."[11] Stevie is the moral barometer of the novel—Conrad's Holy Fool—a truly compassionate character who acts as a foil to the sham revolutionaries and heartless government functionaries. That Conrad would make a character such as this his moral spokesman in the novel reflects his profound pessimism.

COLONIALISM IN *HEART OF DARKNESS*, *LORD JIM*, AND *NOSTROMO*

Heart of Darkness (1899), *Lord Jim* (1900), and *Nostromo* (1904) represent Conrad's most important meditations on colonialism. In *Heart of Darkness*, the narrator, Marlow, witnesses the horrors of Belgian colonialism, culminating in the physical and moral destruction of Kurtz. Kurtz represents the pinnacle of European civilization. A painter, speaker, politician, "universal genius"[12]—"All Europe contributed to the making of Kurtz."[13] His madness and dissolution in the jungle therefore symbolize Europe's debacle in Africa. Marlow notices how natural the Africans themselves appear to be, how at home in their own environment. As he steams along the edge of the continent in a French gunboat, waiting to be dropped at the head of the Congo River, he sees African men paddling closer to shore: "They shouted, sang; their bodies streamed with perspiration; they had faces like grotesque masks—these chaps, but they had bone, muscle, a wild vitality, an intense energy of movement that was as natural and true as the surf along their coast. They wanted no excuse for being there."[14] The most important word in that description might be the pronoun *their*; it was *their* surf, *their* coast, *their* continent. The whites, Marlow suggests, have no excuse for being there; they corrupt the Africans who cooperate with them; they enslave or imprison the rest, and they themselves die of African illnesses at the same time that they are corrupted by their own power.

In *Lord Jim* the protagonist flees to Sulaco in Borneo to escape his identity as a ship's officer who, in a fit of cowardice, leapt from a crippled ship, leaving the helpless passengers to their fates. Despite his failure, he is a dependable, honest young Englishman who is trusted and helped by Marlow, the same character Conrad introduced in *Heart of Darkness*. When he lands in Sulaco as a trader—the only European—Jim sets to work as a colonial administrator, and he soon becomes the trusted leader of the community. But even Jim fails in this colonial role, though he has the best intentions and the help of the most powerful group in Sulaco.

Jim attempts to impose his vision of justice and community on the Malaysians, but he leaves them and their community in chaos at the end.

Nostromo anticipates the indirect colonialism that emerged throughout the world later in the 20th century, after former colonies gained their independence. Holroyd is a great American financier who lives in San Francisco. He is the chief financial backer of the great San Tomé silver mine in Sulaco, a city in Costaguana, Conrad's name for his South American country. Holroyd visits Sulaco and the mine and stays with the man who controls the mine, Charles Gould. Holroyd promises to continue backing Gould, and he says this about the economic role of the United States:

> We [the people of the United States] shall be giving the word for everything: industry, trade, law, journalism, art, politics, and religion, from Cape Horn clear over to Smith's Sound, and beyond, too, if anything worth taking hold of turns up at the North Pole. And then we shall have the leisure to take in hand the outlying islands and continents of the earth. We shall run the world's business whether the world likes it or not. The world can't help it—and neither can we, I guess.[15]

Once again we find an admirable European, the Englishman Charles Gould, who (like Kurtz) is corrupted by the insidious but overwhelming forces of economic imperialism, represented in the novel by Holroyd and symbolized by the San Tomé silver mine. Though the silver is in Costaguana, only a European, Gould, has the knowledge and the ambition (fueled by his idealism and his egotism) to extract it. And the mine corrupts nearly everyone it touches. Like the ivory in Africa, the silver draws Europeans into a world where they simply don't belong.

CONRAD'S DIFFICULTY

Cedric Watts, a fine, contemporary Conrad scholar, wrote this at the beginning of his edition of *Lord Jim*.

> In July 1900, Conrad finished *Lord Jim* at dawn after writing all night. (A mound of cigarette-ends nearby; pages of manuscript blowing about the study in the morning breeze.)

He wrote the last word, went into the dining-room, and shared a piece of cold chicken with his dog. Sixty-one years later, sitting in a sunny back-yard with my feet propped on a dustbin, I ended my first reading of the novel. The blurb on the rear cover of my Penguin text said of Jim: 'No less fascinating than the motives and adventures of this strange personality is Conrad's method of unfolding the story.' I reflected for a while, took up my pen, crossed out 'fascinating' and wrote above it 'infuriating.'[16]

Fifty years later, my own students are even more infuriated, for at least four different reasons. First, reading Conrad's novels requires attention to detail, an appreciation for stylistic subtlety, and, above all, patience—qualities that television and the internet tend to discourage. His fractured chronologies, involved sentences, and sophisticated vocabulary don't invite easy and rapid reading. Second, readers must confront what might be perceived to be misogyny in his earlier work—evident in *An Outcaste of the Islands* (1896), *Heart of Darkness*, and *Lord Jim*. Women have limited roles in most British and American adventure fiction—they most often represent the smothering voice of convention that men flee to seek their adventures in the first place; they are objects to be won or merely protected, or even subtle but dangerous foes. These are the roles that women have in Conrad's early tales of adventure. Third, we must decide how to respond to the charges of racism leveled against some of his work, and this can make both teachers and students uncomfortable. One of Conrad's early long tales is entitled "The Nigger of the *Narcissus*." Some readers will find it easier simply not to read that story than to deal with its title and its depiction of the doomed Black man who haunts it. Fourth and finally, readers must confront the darkness of his novels and stories. Conrad rejected all political and economic systems—monarchic, socialist, democratic, or fascist, and he distrusted all philosophies. In *Heart of Darkness*, Marlow dismisses the belief that people can rely on ideas and principles to motivate them or to keep them morally straight: "Principles won't do," he says. Principles are merely "Acquisitions, clothes, pretty rags—rags that would fly off at the first good shake."[17] Conrad's pessimism (some might call it "nihilism") and irony are unrelenting, and some readers might prefer to leave him, so to speak, in the 20th century.

But I believe, and I have found, that the struggle is well worth it. No one (with the possible exception of Conrad's friend, H.G. Wells) anticipated the evils of the 20th century as accurately as Conrad. I have argued elsewhere that Conrad's depictions of the "brick maker" in *Heart of Darkness* and of Hirsch in *Nostromo* are proof of a certain degree of anti-Semitism.[18] Yet the torture and murder of Hirsch, a Jewish merchant, described in *Nostromo* eerily anticipates the cruelty of governments in the 20th century and, especially, the Nazis' "Final Solution" that led to the Holocaust. And Conrad's exploration of unbridled, arbitrary state power in that novel and in *Under Western Eyes* is unparalleled. *The Secret Agent* and *Under Western Eyes* anticipate the cruelty inherent within the radical political philosophies—both Fascism and Marxism—that grew out of the turn of the 19th century. *Heart of Darkness* and *Nostromo* are the greatest fictional depictions and, ultimately, condemnations of colonialism in Africa and South America of their time. Francis Ford Copolla's brilliant adaptation of *Heart of Darkness* in *Apocalypse Now* confirms its universality. Conrad's career even anticipated the emergence of feminism—he began with the traditional, patriarchal attitudes expressed in *Heart of Darkness* and ended with an acknowledgement of women's oppression and a subtle but unmistakable critique of patriarchy in *The Secret Agent*, *Under Western Eyes*, and *Victory* (1915).

In short, for those willing to accept the challenge, no 20th century author is more rewarding.

NOTES

1. In his fine biography of Conrad, Zdzislaw Najder writes on p. 166: "Intentionally or not, Bobrowski did a great deal to impede Konrad's understanding of his father. His Uncle Tadeusz's stories and opinions must have left Konrad with the impression that Apollo had been an irresponsible fanatic who had ruined the life of his loving wife."

2. Najder, 51-52.

3. John Batchelor, *The Life of Joseph Conrad*, (Oxford, UK: Blackwell, 1994): 29-37.

4. Joseph Conrad, *Nostromo: A Tale of the Seaboard*. Keith Carabine, ed. (Oxford, UK: Oxford U P, 1984).

5. Chinua Achebe, "An Image of Africa: Racism in Conrad's *Heart of Darkness*." Rpt. in *Heart of Darkness: An Authoritative Text: Backgrounds and Sources: Criticism*. 3rd ed. Robert Kimbrough, ed. (New York: Norton, 1988): 257, 259.

6. Eloise Knapp Hay, "Joseph Conrad and Impressionism." *Journal-of-Aesthetics-and-Art-Criticism*, 34 (1975): 137.

7. Ian Watt. *Conrad in the 19th Century*. (Berkeley: U of California P, 1979): 169-80.

8. *Heart of Darkness: An Authoritative Text*: Backgrounds and Sources: Criticism. Cited above: 45-6.

9. *Heart of Darkness: An Authoritative Text*: 62.

10. Joseph Conrad, *Lord Jim*. Ed. Cedric Watts & Robert Hampson (New York: Penguin, 1987): 199.

11. Joseph Conrad, *The Secret Agent: A Simple Tale*. (Garden City, NY: Doubleday, 1953): 145, 146.

12. *Heart of Darkness*, 30.

13. *Heart of Darkness*, 50.

14. *Heart of Darkness*, 17.

15. Joseph Conrad, *Nostromo: A Tale of the Seaboard* (Oxford: Oxford U P, 1995): 77.

16. Cedric Watts, "Introduction" to *Lord Jim* (Middlesex, UK: Penguin, 1949): 11.

17. *Heart of Darkness*, 38.

18. Richard Ruppel, "*Lord Jim*'s Marlow and the French Lieutenant: Mapping Conrad's Ethnocentrism." *L'Epoque Conradienne*, pp. 79-86. (Société Conradienne Française, 1990): 82-83.

CAROLA M. KAPLAN

Colonizers, Cannibals, and the Horror of Good Intentions in Joseph Conrad's Heart of Darkness

"Man can embody truth but he cannot know it." Nowhere is William Butler Yeats's adage more clearly illustrated than in the narrative of Charlie Marlow in *Heart of Darkness*. Throughout the text, Marlow insists upon the distinction between truth and lies; between men and women; between civilization and savagery; and, most of all, between Self and Other. Of these, the most important distinction is between Self and Other, for it is this opposition that sustains the colonial enterprise. The lure and the fear of the Other initiate the pursuit and "discovery" of colonialism; the conviction of the inferiority of the Other justifies the undertaking. Yet despite Marlow's insistence, all binary oppositions collapse in the course of his narrative: colonists prove to be conquerors, the gang of virtue is indistinguishable from the gang of greed, the illusions of women merely echo the illusions of men, and there is no clear distinction between lies and truth. Most importantly, the fundamental difference between Self and Other disappears and, with it, the unbridgeable gulf between men and women and between savage and civilized that sustains the power structure of western civilization. But this awareness offered by the text eludes Marlow for, enmeshed in his own culture, he would find this awareness "too dark—too dark altogether."

From *Studies in Short Fiction* 34 (1997): 323-33. © 1997 by *Studies in Short Fiction*. Reprinted by permission.

67

In psychological terms, the Other is but the undiscovered territory in the self. In the colonial enterprise, this territory of the unconscious is displaced onto another people who both allure and terrify. The colonizer, fearing to succumb to the Other, attempts to contain it—through subordination, suppression, or conversion. These strategies of containment are designed to preserve the opposition and inequality between Self and Other that justifies the imperialist enterprise. The central trope of imperialism is what Abdul R. JanMohamed terms "the Manichean allegory" that converts racial difference "into, moral and even metaphysical difference" (80). This allegory characterizes the relationship between dominant and subordinate culture as one of ineradicable opposition (82). Although the opposing terms of the allegory change—good and evil, civilization and savagery, intelligence and emotion, rationality and sensuality—they are always predicated upon the assumption of the superiority of the outside evaluator and the inferiority of the native being observed.

Colonialist literature, as byproduct of the imperialist enterprise, necessarily reinscribes the Manichean allegory either to confirm or to interrogate it in an effort to move beyond its limits. As a result, colonialist texts take two forms, which reflect, respectively, these two different responses: the "imaginary" and the "symbolic" (JanMohamed 84). These designations derive from Jacques Lacan's descriptions of sequential stages of human development. The "imaginary," according to Lacan, dates from the mirror stage of infant life, in which the child of six to eighteen months jubilantly identifies itself with its mirror image, the wholeness and integrity of which belie the internal flux and fragmentation the child experiences (Lacan 4). Because of the unbridgeable distance of the specular image with which the child identifies, the child situates within it rivalry, opposition, and aggressivity (Gallop 59). The relation between the self and its image, which Lacan terms "the imaginary," is one in which mirroring forestalls inter-subjectivity or the interaction between two separate selves, each with its own distinct perspective.

In the "imaginary" colonialist text, JanMohamed observes, "the native functions as an image of the imperialist self in such a manner that it reveals the latter's self-alienation" (84). This self-alienation consists in the failure to recognize as inherent within the self despised attributes the imperialist projects onto the Other. Thus, the "imaginary" colonialist text adheres to a fixed opposition between the self and the native, insisting upon the homogeneous identity of the indigenous population and taking refuge in the "superior," more "enlightened," and more "civilized" perspective of the dominant culture. Interpreted through the narrative perspective of Marlow, *Heart of Darkness* exemplifies the "imaginary" colonialist text.

The second type of colonialist fiction, the "symbolic," parallels the stage at which the young child, once having become convinced of its wholeness and integrity, is able to recognize and identify with an imago or subject-image as a counterpart; and is then able to enter into a dialectic that links the self or I "with socially elaborated situations" (Lacan 5). At this stage, the child is able to enter into social exchange, dialogue, and relationship (Gallop 59–61). An equivalent stage in culture would make possible a dialectic encounter between Self and Other in which the dominant culture is able to bracket its own values and thus radically to question its basis for cultural inference and interpretation. Such a dialectic or exchange would aim at resolving cultural oppositions through syncretic solutions (JanMohamed 85). Such, I would argue, is the larger narrative perspective of *Heart of Darkness*, which exposes the limitations and self-contradiction of Marlow's views to open up a complex dialogue on issues of history, culture, race, and gender. Thus the entirety of *Heart of Darkness* attempts to deal with the Other in symbolic terms, although Marlow is able to deal with the Other only in the realm of the Imaginary.

Heart of Darkness points to awarenesses beyond Marlow both by revealing his limitations and by systematically undercutting the polarities and distinctions that Marlow takes pains to establish. From the first, Marlow's narrative invites the reader to reach an understanding beyond him when he states that his experience was "not very clear. And yet it seemed to throw a kind of light" (70). Among his many limitations in dealing with cultural differences, Marlow displays his xenophobia when he reluctantly accepts his relatives' choice of living on the Continent, explaining, "It's cheap and not so nasty as it looks, they say" (71). Further, he exhibits contradictory ideas about entering another culture, revealing his determination to get to Africa "by hook or by crook" but, once there, feeling like "an imposter" (77) when he observes that the natives (unlike him) "wanted no excuse for being there" (78). He insists that he detests and avoids lies, yet acknowledges three separate lies in the course of the narrative—to the station manager, to Kurtz, and to the Intended. He maintains that the conquest of the earth is redeemed by "an unselfish belief in the idea—something you can set up, and bow down before, and offer a sacrifice to" (69–70). Not only is this assertion undercut by the language of idolatry, but it prefigures evidence, as the narrative unfolds, that Kurtz' belief in the idea of "humanizing, improving, instructing" (101) leads to the most ruthless exploitation and most appalling idolatry of all, as Kurtz turns himself, the emissary of the idea, into all object of worship. Further, Marlow dismisses as foolish his aunt's notion of "weaning those ignorant millions from their horrid ways" (76), but describes as "a beautiful piece of writing" Kurtz' kindred assertion, "By the simple exercise of our will we can exert a power for good [among the natives] practically unbounded" (123). Throughout the text, Marlow works hard to separate savage customs from civilized behavior, yet an observer might be pressed to distinguish Marlow's noisy jig with the boiler-maker (when he finally gets rivets to repair his boat) (98) from the "whirl of black limbs" (105) on shore that he condescends to regard as "not inhuman" (105). Similarly, Marlow's distinction between the comprehensible language of civilized discourse and the incomprehensible noise of savages—"the roll of drums" (105), "abrupt burst of yells" (141), "savage clamour" (113), "savage discords" (110), "tumultuous and mournful uproar" (110)—breaks down. All voices, European and native, degenerate in Marlow's memory into "one immense jabber, silly, atrocious, sordid, savage, or simply mean, without any kind of sense" (120–21).

Because most of Marlow's attempts at separations prove unstable and many of his distinctions blur, they serve to reveal his intense need to sustain the Manichean allegory so necessary to his sense of Self in contradistinction to the Other. Underlying Marlow's efforts to maintain binary oppositions is the colonizer's intense anxiety about being taken over by the Other. Marlow's strategy of containment emerges most forcefully throughout the text in his parallel descriptions of women and of natives.[1]

Throughout his account, Marlow both denigrates and over-estimates the power of women. Through synecdoche, Marlow reduces the women he sees in the waiting room of the Belgian shipping company to "one fat and the other slim" (73), one young and one old, "knitting black wool as for a warm pall" (74). At the same time, they are oddly "uncanny and fateful" (74); and Marlow after his encounter with Kurtz observes, "the knitting old woman with the cat obtruded herself upon my memory as a most improper person to be sitting at the other end of such an affair" (142). Analogously, the secretary, who seems to know all about Marlow's fate, he reduces to "a white-haired secretarial head, but wearing a compassionate expression" (74).

Similarly, Marlow downplays his aunt's power, while inadvertently revealing his reliance upon her. After disavowing his dependency on women—"Then—would you believe it? ... I, Charlie Marlow, set the women to work—to get a job. Heavens!"—he acknowledges that he relied upon his aunt to get him the job as captain of the Congo steamer. His aunt, who clearly wields more social power than Marlow, he describes patronizingly as "a dear enthusiastic soul" (76), although her influential recommendations of him haunt him along his Congo journey and serve to ally him with the similarly "gifted" Kurtz. As he describes her, he confines his aunt to a drawing room "that most soothingly looked just as you would expect a lady's drawing room to look" (76), a description that contrasts markedly with his later description of the disquieting drawing room in which he encounters Kurtz' Intended. Marlow's adverb "soothingly" suggests his discomfort at the idea of encountering a woman who is not contained in a drawing room, a discomfort he will experience at its most extreme in his meeting with the "savage" woman in the jungle. Once he returns from the Congo, no lady's drawing room will again be a "soothing" place because he will have found out—although he never consciously admits it—that neither women nor domestic space offer sanctuary from the knowledge of the pervasiveness of evil.

Marlow's self-deluding ability to polarize his experiences—in particular, to separate the "soothing" female world of illusions from the larger male world of shocking realities—collapses in his interview with the Intended. Despite Marlow's efforts to keep these worlds separate, after his jungle encounter with Kurtz, they fuse in the nightmare atmosphere of the Intended's drawing room, inhabited by Kurtz' ghost, whose words echo and eerily combine with hers to form the ghastly chorus Marlow hears. This chorus suggests a terrifying intertwining of purpose between Kurtz and his Intended—a collusion between the "soul as translucently pure as a cliff of crystal" (149) and the "soul that knew no restraint, no faith, and no fear" (144). For this reason, when Marlow asserts, "I saw them together—I heard them together" (154) in the drawing room, he experiences "a sensation of panic in my heart as though I had blundered into a place of cruel and absurd mysteries not fit for a human being to behold" (154). (The phrase "cruel and absurd mysteries" eerily echoes the "unspeakable rites" attributed to Kurtz in Africa). In this scene, Marlow's language and observations suggest, although his panic and confusion indicate he does not consciously understand, that domestic bliss and female innocence in Belgium are predicated upon the exploitation of natives and the pilfering of ivory in the Congo; that marriages between ambitious young men of insufficient means with young women of substance are facilitated by the colonial enterprise, in which enterprising young men make good in the name of doing good. ("I had heard that her engagement with Kurtz had been disapproved by her people. He wasn't rich enough or something ... He had given me some reason to infer that it was his impatience of comparative poverty that drove him out there" [155]).

Many apparently innocent features of the drawing room recall sinister aspects of the colonial enterprise presented earlier in the story. Thus, the grand piano "like a sombre and polished sarcophagus" (153) recalls the image of Brussels, the city outside her door, site of the colonial Company's offices, as "a whited sepulchre" (73); the piano, symbol of feminine refinement, has keys of ivory, the ivory Kurtz pilfered from Africa; the apparently noble image of the Intended's white forehead "illumined by the unextinguishable light of belief and love" (154) against the dark background of the room recalls Kurtz's ominous painting of her "draped and blindfolded, carrying a torch" in which "the effect of the torch-light on the face was sinister" (92). In the drawing room scene, she is in effect blindfolded by her enduring and willful illusions about Kurtz and she carries the torch of his ideas, which cast a sinister light back upon her. Fittingly, the image of her hair as an "ashy halo" associates her apparently angelic goodness with death. Consequently Marlow, in acknowledging that the Intended's claim, "I knew him best" (107), may be accurate, aptly notes that "with every word spoken the room was growing darker" (107)—that is, more unfathomable, more remote from truth, more connected with evil, more suggestive of death. In this scene all details combine to point out that domestic innocence colludes with global evil in death-dealing conspiracy. Yet, in the Intended's drawing room, as in other stations along his pilgrimage, Marlow shrinks from the enormity of the knowledge he is offered.

Similarly, in his descriptions of the African natives, as in his glib generalizations about women, Marlow likewise attempts to deny the power of the Other he fears by resorting to stereotypes. Just as his descriptions of women are reductive, so too are his accounts of the natives, whom he acknowledges only. in generic descriptions. "Dark human shapes could be made out in the distance.... two bronze figures, leaning on tall spears, stood in the sunlight under fantastic head-dresses of spotted skins, warlike and still in statuesque repose" (136). Even when described individually, they are stereotyped: "The man seemed young— almost a boy—but you know with them it's hard to tell" (82). Marlow's stereotypical descriptions of both women and natives serve a strategy of containment that enables him to deny both their importance for him and his affinity with them.

Nowhere, however, is Marlow's containment of the Other through discourse so sustained as in his treatment of the "savage" woman, the figure in which race and gender emblematically intersect. This is not to say that racial and sexual difference are to be equated. Since the value attributed to each is culturally determined, interpretations of racial and sexual superiority vary from one culture to another; and within any particular culture these constructions may conflict rather than intersect. Yet when *Heart of Darkness* presents an African tribal culture that reverses both the racial and sexual hierarchy of the West, these reversals constitute a powerful double threat to Western social constructions that Marlow views as natural and inevitable.[2]

Marlow's compelling but ambivalent description of the "savage" woman enables the reader to see the contrast between her authority and unique attributes and Marlow's repeated attempts, throughout the text, to deny the power and individuality of African natives. Marlow responds to her dangerous allure—dangerous because he sees her as partly responsible for Kurtz's "going native"—by insisting on her ineradicable twofold otherness, the savage and female as distinguished from the civilized and male. By designating her the living embodiment of these dualities, Marlow shores up the binary oppositions upon which his understanding of Western civilization rests.

The "savage" woman, as Marlow describes her, is a distillation of alluring but frightening otherness. His view of her highlights her beauty, leadership, and ferocity. She is "wild," "gorgeous" (136), and proud. Wearing a helmet, armor, and magic charms, she is fearless in the face of the pilgrims' bullets, and is obeyed by her tribesmen. She is "like the wilderness itself, with an air of brooding over an inscrutable purpose" (137), a description sufficiently ominous but all the more so for echoing the previous description of the wilderness as "an implacable force brooding over an inscrutable intention" (103). Although she is without words, the "savage" woman is not without purpose—and this, her "struggling, half-shaped resolve" (137), is all the more menacing for being unknowable. Her threatening otherness is most fully articulated by Marlow's parodic double, the Russian "man of patches" (88) who finds her so frightening that he proclaims: "If she had offered to come aboard [the steamer] I really think I would have tried to shoot her" (88). The contrast between the harlequin's nervousness and the "savage" woman's composure, between his ragged attire and her "gorgeous" adornment highlights her formidable power.

In her overt sexuality and aggressive claims upon Kurtz's person, Marlow finds her both enticing and menacing. Voracious and diabolical, she appears to belong to a matriarchal and polyandrous female warrior culture. Equated with the wilderness—she is its "tenebrous and passionate soul" (137)—she is a kind of succubus that has made Kurtz her concubine and thereby drained him of his vitality:

> The wilderness had patted him on the head.... it had caressed him, and—lo!—he had withered; it had taken him, loved him, embraced him, got into his veins, consumed his flesh, and sealed his soul to its own by the inconceivable ceremonies of some devilish initiation. He was its spoiled and pampered favourite (121).

The "savage" woman is one with the wilderness that has claimed Kurtz for its harem. This image of Kurtz as the "spoiled and pampered favourite" in a male harem directly threatens the patriarchal and ostensibly monogamous structure of the society from which he has emigrated.

So threatening is the "savage" woman in her sexual otherness that Marlow adopts a strategy of subduing her power through grief: "she stopped as if her heart had failed her" (137). Finally the text supplants her with—in effect, turns her into—the Intended, in perpetual mourning and domestic confinement, whose outstretched arms mirror the "savage" woman's gesture but lack her power to command a tribe or to enshroud a pilgrim ship in shadow: "Suddenly she [the "savage" woman] opened her bared arms and threw them up rigid above her head.... and at the same time the swift shadows darted out on the earth, swept around on the river, gathering the steamer into a shadowy embrace" (88). Thus Marlow's narration quells the anxiety the "savage" woman evokes: It demonstrates that her "barbarous" charms are in fact "powerless" (156). Her inconsolable grief, in paralyzing her, restores the male—in the person of her paramour, Kurtz—to primacy.

The colonialist anxiety of being taken over by the Other surfaces even more frighteningly in the cannibalism that Marlow imputes to the native workers aboard his boat who, at any moment, may devour Marlow and the pilgrims. In *Heart of Darkness*, cannibalism serves as the metaphor for the absolute violation of boundaries between one human being and another, the physical equivalent of the cultural absorption or ingestion by the Other that the colonizer fears.

On another level, the cannibalism Marlow imputes to the natives may be merely a guilty projection of the rapacity of the white colonizers who, as Jonathan Swift noted about earlier British colonial exploiters in "A Modest Proposal," have already devoured the native population in less literal ways. Since the European intruders have invaded territorial boundaries, have violated property rights, and have in fact confiscated the natives' most personal property—their bodies—for their own uses, the Europeans are but one step from literally devouring the inhabitants. In fact, Marlow describes the insatiable Kurtz as threatening to do so: "I saw him open his mouth wide—it gave him a weirdly voracious aspect, as though he had wanted to swallow all the air, all the earth, all the men before him" (135). Even Marlow's approval of the apparent restraint of the natives aboard ship, whom he takes to be hungry cannibals, may simply suggest the guilt he feels at the Europeans' lack of restraint toward the indigenous population.

Marlow's attribution of cannibalism to the natives—an accusation never borne out by their behavior—is a violence Marlow inflicts on the culture. This violence is characteristic of all linguistic descriptions of the members of one culture by members of another culture who exercise power over them and exploit them. Throughout, *Heart of Darkness*

suggests that physical violence originates in the violence of language—
the language that is used to justify intrusion, usurpation, and conversion.
As Jacques Derrida observes, human violence originates in the violence
of the letter, which takes many forms:[3] in *Heart of Darkness*, the map of
Africa, divided and colored according to the greedy claims of European
nations; the inscription upon the land of roads and railroads; the delivery
of mail from home to European intruders; the keeping of accounts to
tally the loot; the written recommendations of outsiders to legitimize the
coercion of natives; the Bible that justifies the pilgrims in converting and
(if resisted) in killing the natives; and the law that labels some natives
"enemies" and others "criminals" and thereby legitimizes clapping them
in irons and forcing them into chain gangs. Thus Marlow correctly
describes Kurtz primarily as a "voice" whose "unextinguishable gift of
noble and lofty expression" (146) authorizes and smoothes the way for
indulging his consummate greed.[4] The text suggests the inevitable
course of Kurtz's report to the International Society for the Suppression
of Savage Customs that begins by arguing that the godlike status of
white men in the Congo enables them to "exert a power for good
practically unbounded" and ends by urging "Exterminate all the brutes!"
(123). As Marlow ironically yet revealingly suggests, this last admonition
"may be regarded as the exposition of a method."

The text's recognition of the violence inherent in language also
helps to explain the narrative event most puzzling to critics, Marlow's
apparent lie to Kurtz's Intended. In reply to her request for "His last
word—to live with," Marlow responds, "The last word he pronounced
was—your name." By this assertion, Marlow inadvertently tells her the
truth. For Kurtz, the Intended is not a distinct person. Just as she has no
name of her own, she has no intrinsic reality for Kurtz. She is the
expression of his intentions, of the life he intends for her, one that
reflects his culture-based ideas about marriage, sexuality, and the
subordination of women. She is, in effect, colonized by Kurtz's
intentions, which confine her in the drawing room and limit her
discourse to an echo of his.

Similarly, the African natives exist in the text as expressions of
Kurtz's—and Marlow's—intentions. They exist for Kurtz's uses and are
confined to Marlow's conceptions of them. To have intentions toward a
people is to appropriate for oneself the right to subdue, to convert, and
to use—all in the name of benevolence. Thus "the horror" is indeed the

name of the Intended: it designates the violence that results from the intentions of the powerful who impose their will upon the powerless.[5]

Further, the designation "the Intended" signals an awareness that permeates the text of the unreliability and slipperiness of language. "The Intended" is the shifting signifier, sign of the unbridgeable gulf between aim and achievement, the gap in meaning that cannot be sutured. Without heeding the text's warning about the unreliable and equivocal nature of language, the reader may trust too much to Marlow's words, just as Kurtz' adherents have trusted too much to his eloquence; and potential colonist-conquerors may fool themselves as well as others into believing in their noble intentions. Repeatedly, in recording the booming voice but essential hollowness of Kurtz, the text underlines the tricky nature of language itself that conceals as it apparently reveals, that denotes presence while signifying absence, that signals meaning while lacking it.

By the time Marlow tells the truth he considers a lie when he suggests that "the horror" is the name of Kurtz' Intended (that is to say, the name for what he had intended), the text has effectually blurred the distinction between truth and lies, much as it has blurred the distinctions between colonists and conquerors, between savagery and civilization, between men's realities and women's illusions.

If, as has often been claimed, Marlow represents a white, patriarchal, Eurocentric view of late nineteenth-century history,[6] the text suggests, although it does not develop, a perspective on contemporary global politics that is more complex and more problematic than Marlow's. Unlike Marlow's conflation of all historic periods into one universal time and his insistence that Africa mirrors the beginnings of Western civilization, the text marks a specific moment in the European imperialist enterprise, the moment in which late nineteenth-century England, disconcertingly akin to the more overtly ruthless Belgium, was frantically grabbing territory in outlying regions of the world. Unlike Marlow's erasure of class differences through his creation of an artificially egalitarian community aboard a yacht (in which a plain seaman rubs elbows with a lawyer and a director of companies), the text recognizes that even in the jungle class barriers exist between colonial officials and working men, such as mechanics and boiler-makers.

Further, although Marlow posits an essential and innate ideological difference between men and women, the text recognizes that late-Victorian society assigns very limited roles to women so that, if their social views are unrealistic, it is because they lack education and therefore merely echo male platitudes. In addition, the text briefly notices—in the dress and status of the "savage" woman and in the dialect of her tribe—the particularities of a specific African tribal culture and recognizes that this culture has language and meaning, while observing that these are unreadable to outsiders. Thus Marlow's dying helmsman appears to want to speak but cannot do so to those who do not and will not understand him (119).

Finally, the narrative stipulates that what it arbitrarily equates with darkness is in fact universal—an ineradicable core of evil in all human beings, whatever their culture of origin. When Marlow observes about modern England, "And this also ... has been one of the dark places of the earth" (67), his use of the perfect tense brings his observation into the present. By the time Marlow ceases to speak to his audience on the "cruising yawl," symbolically the privileged site of the dominant culture, all persons on board must acknowledge that the apparently "tranquil waterway" of modern European history leads "into the heart of an immense darkness" (158), located not only in the outposts of empire but always already within the human breast.

NOTES

1. These display "an imperialism of the metaphor rooted in a patriarchal language that conflates racial difference with sexual difference in the field of Western representations" (McGee 130).

2. For persuasive discussions of the difference between sexual and racial alterity and of the need to distinguish clearly between them, see Spivak, Mohanty and Suleri.

3. Noting that all language is violence, speech as well as writing, Jacques Derrida makes the point that "the essential confrontation that opens communication between peoples and cultures, even when that communication is not practiced under the banner of colonial or missionary oppression," takes the form of war (107). As examples of violent inscription, Derrida cites the road, the path, and other instances of the opening and spacing of nature (107–08).

4. Jacques Derrida warns of the dangers of phonologism, "the exclusion or abasement of writing" (102). Phonologism privileges speech

over writing because of an erroneous belief that speech is originary and therefore naturally more innocent than writing (106). Perhaps the greatest danger of phonologism is that the eloquent speaker—such as Kurtz—persuades his audience by appearing to stand in for the presence that words necessarily lack.

5. For previous discussions that suggest that "the Horror" is the name of the Intended, although they interpret the horror she represents in different ways than I do, see Bruffee, Ellis, Kauvar, Stark, and Milne. Of all these interpretations, mine is closest to that of Stark, who maintains that the Intended is herself a "whited sepulchre." Stark, however, goes further than I do in his dire assessment of the Intended: he asserts that the house of the Intended is the "symbolic center of the Inner Circle of the Infernal System" (543), that is, the inner center of Hell; and that the Intended's glittering eyes signal her infernal character, which manifests itself in part through her seduction and manipulation of Marlow.

6. For fuller discussions of Marlow as embodiment of the ideology of European imperialism, see Said 48; Brantlinger 173–97; and McGee 127–32.

Works Cited

Brantlinger, Patrick. *Rule of Darkness: British Literature and Imperialism, 1830–1914*. Ithaca: Cornell UP, 1988.

Conrad, Joseph. *Heart of Darkness*. New York: New American Library, 1950.

Bruffee, David. "The Lesser Nightmare: Marlow's Lie in *Heart of Darkness*." *Modern Language Quarterly* 25 (1964): 322–29.

Derrida, Jacques. *Of Grammatology*. Trans. Gayatri Chakravorty Spivak. Baltimore: Johns Hopkins UP, 1976.

Ellis, James. "Kurtz's Voice: The Intended as 'The Horror.'" *English Literature in Transition 1880–1920* 19 (1976): 105–10.

Gallop, Jane. *Reading Lacan*. Ithaca: Cornell UP, 1985.

JanMohamed, Abdul R. "The Economy of Manichean Allegory: The Function of Racial Difference in Colonialist Literature." *"Race," Writing, and Difference*. Ed. Henry Louis Gates, Jr. Chicago: U of Chicago P, 1986. 78–106.

Kauvar, Gerald B. "Marlow as Liar." *Studies in Short Fiction* 5 (1968): 290–92;

Lacan, Jacques. "The Mirror Stage as Formative of the Function of the I." *Écrits: A Selection*. Trans. Alan Sheridan. New York: Norton, 1977. 1–7.

McGee, Patrick. *Telling the Other: The Question of Value in Modern and Postcolonial Writing*. Ithaca, New York: Cornell UP, 1992.

Milne, Fred L. "Marlow's Lie and the Intended: Civilization as the Lie in *Heart of Darkness*." *Arizona Quarterly* 44 (1985): 106–12.

Mohanty, Chandra. "Under Western Eyes: Feminist Scholarship and Colonial Discourses." *Colonial Discourse and Post-Colonial Theory*. Ed. Patrick Williams and Laura Chrisman. New York: Columbia UP, 1994. 196–220.

Said, Edward W. "Intellectuals in the Post-Colonial World." *Salmagundi* 70–71 (1986): 44–81.

Spivak, Gayatri Chakravorty. "Can the Subaltern Speak?" *Marxism and the Interpretation of Culture*. Eds. Cary Nelson and Lawrence Grossberg. Urbana: U of Illinois P, 1988. 271–313.

Stark, Bruce R. "Kurtz's Intended: The Heart of *Heart of Darkness*." *Texas Studies in Literature and Language* 16 (1974): 535–55.

Suleri, Sara. "Woman Skin Deep: Feminism and the Postcolonial Condition." *Colonial Discourse and Post-Colonial Theory*. Eds. Patrick Williams and Laura Chrisman. New York: Columbia UP, 1994. 244–56.

DAVID ALLEN WARD

"An Ideal Conception": Conrad's Nostromo and the Problem of Identity

More than one critic has commented that in *Nostromo* Joseph Conrad sacrifices detailed psychological analysis in his effort to create a work of considerable social and historical scope. According to this view, the breadth of Conrad's undertaking in the novel, which he himself referred to as his "largest canvas," effectively precludes a thorough exploration of individual mental experience. F. R. Leavis was among the first to note that the work does not concern itself greatly with "the inner complexities of the individual psyche."[1] Its power, he asserts, lies rather "in the vivid reality of the things we are made to see and hear, and the significance they get from their relations in a highly organized and vividly realized whole."[2]

That *Nostromo* is a novel full of much external "action"—murder, suicide, theft, escape, capture, and political intrigue—is certainly indisputable, as is the fact that the narrative is not centered in the affairs of any single character, the title of the work notwithstanding. Indeed, it is for some critics a novel on the grandest scales. For Robert Penn Warren, for example, the novel is a "great, massive, multiphase symbol" that renders Conrad's "total vision of the world, his sense of individual destiny, his sense of man's place in nature, his sense of history and society."[3] But as far-reaching as the work's social and historical implications may be, implications that have been examined at length by

From *Conradiana: A Journal of Joseph Conrad Studies* 35:3 (1992). © 1992 by *Conradiana*. Reprinted by permission.

a host of critics, the novel is not without its significance to the issue of human psychology. It is certainly not as far removed from the drama of personal mental experience, that is, the interior lives of the characters, as Leavis and others suggest.

The narrative explores in its development of four major characters—Charles Gould, Dr. Monygham, Nostromo, and Martin Decoud—as well as in its development of lesser figures, the process of identity formation. It delineates how these individuals adopt certain external, idealized images of themselves as a means of functioning in the human community, the microcosm of Costaguana—that little world of Sulaco and its environs, sealed off from the outside by the Golfo Placido and the towering Cordillera. Conrad's conception of human identity, as revealed in *Nostromo*, bears striking resemblance to the ideas of French thinker Jacques Lacan, who in his noted mirror stage theory describes the role of the ideal in the construction of personal identity. Demonstrating that resemblance is the central concern of this essay.

As readers of Lacan well know, the moment in which an infant first recognizes his own image in a mirror is significant not just as a specific phase in child psychology, an actual event that occurs between the ages of six and eighteen months, but as an illustration of what this theorist sees as a permanent tendency of the human personality. Just as the young child joyously sees himself as unified and autonomous, although he is actually, in Lacan's words, "still sunk in his motor incapacity and nursling dependence,"[4] the adult tends throughout life to embrace an ideal image of himself that has no basis in reality. In the Lacanian view of identity formation—one apparently shared by the author of *Nostromo*—the self is invariably founded upon an illusion. Humans are fated to live "outside" themselves, to be prisoners of an external and imaginary ideal image.[5] Lacan speaks of "identification with the Other," for the form that defines the self always comes from without; it is always something added, something artificial—a rigid "armour" that one presents to the world. Thus, in his somber scheme, to be fully human is to delude oneself, the process that creates identity for the self inevitably leads to alienation, for the ideal represented by the projected image is always an unattainable one.

If in the Lacanian perspective, the individual seeks to create an identity by appropriating some external object, in *Nostromo* Charles Gould's obsession with the San Tomé mine can be seen as an effort at self-definition: the mine is the "Other" through which he hopes to achieve an idealized conception of himself. Aaron Fogel even suggests that in using the word "mine" Conrad is engaging in some subtle word play. It designates, of course, the source of the silver, the central image of the novel, but it is also a personal pronoun. When Gould refers to the valuable concession inherited through his father, he can speak of what is "mine"; it is a thing of private ownership. His attempt to realize a sense of self in becoming "master of the mine"—a reading with clear textual support—makes him, in Fogel's opinion, a pitiable figure: "Charles Gould is not so much a great character as a great image of the tragic illusion in the idea that character is self-possession."[6]

Interestingly, early on in the novel, it is Gould's lack of a clearly defined identity—at least in terms of his national status—that is repeatedly emphasized. He is Sulacan by birth, we are told, but strikingly English in appearance. Upon his return to his native Costaguana, it is the reclamation of the silver works that becomes the driving passion of his life, and the text makes clear that this endeavor takes on a deeply personal meaning for him. By making the mine operable he can clearly distinguish his life from that of his father, who was destroyed by the mine. The tragedy of the Gould Concession in his father's life haunts him, and this memory, "closely affecting his own identity, filled his breast with a mournful and angry desire for action."[7] He agrees to the "uncompromising terms" proposed by Holroyd, his North American financier, because through them "the mine preserved its identity, ... and it remained dependent on himself alone."[8] Gould, the narrator observes, "felt that the worthiness of his life was bound up with [the] success" of the silver mine.[9] In a sense, he becomes the mine, living for nothing else and equating its establishment on a sound footing with the construction of a personal identity he desires for himself. The San Tomé mountain, an image of which adorns the "plastered white walls" of the Casa Gould (in much the same way that a lithograph of the worshiped Garibaldi decorates the home of political idealist Giorgio Viola), is productive, then, not just of silver, but of a sense of a unified and autonomous self.

The passages in *Nostromo* that present an anthropomorphized view of the mine take on added significance when read in relationship to Gould's attempts at self-creation. Like his friend Henry James, who in the sinister Gilbert Osmond of *Portrait of a Lady* portrays a character who treats women as objects, using marriage to define himself—Joseph Wiesenfarth calls him a "classic Lacanian example of someone after an object"[10]—Conrad reveals Gould's "identification with the Other" through marriage. Only in Gould's case, his efforts to realize an identity are demonstrated not through an objectifying of his wife Emilia, but in his replacing of her as a spouse with a literal object, the silver mine itself. His gradual absorption in the affairs of the mine is cast as a "subtle conjugal infidelity"; the mine becomes his "mistress,"[11] a beautiful possession that meets his emotional and psychological needs as a kind of surrogate wife. Young Gould enjoys, we are told, not the pleasures of "womankind," but rather "the inseparable companionship of the mine";[12] his preoccupation with the mining operations in Costaguana constitutes a spiritual adultery of which his real spouse Emilia—and others—is all too aware: "The latest phase in the history of the mine Mrs. Gould knew from personal experience. It was in essence the history of her married life."[13] In his letter to his sister, Martin Decoud tells of Gould's "seduction" to an idea; his wife "has discovered that he lives for the mine rather than for her."[14]

Thus, in the same way that James's Isabel Archer can be seen as the Lacanian Other through which Osmond attempts to define himself—to realize a desired self image—the San Tomé mine can be construed as the object Gould embraces in his delusive hope for an ideal identity. To be sure, Gould sees the successful establishment of the mine as working a positive good for the country as a whole, as evidenced in his often-quoted remarks justifying material interests on the basis of the improved conditions they produce for the nation. But, to use the words of Dorothy Van Ghent, "all this—law and order, good faith, security and justice for an oppressed people—is merely incidental to Gould's personal obsession,"[15] an obsession so strong he would rather blow up the mine than see it pass into someone else's hands.

If the flow of silver from the mountain fails to produce the peace and happiness Gould envisions for Costaguana—social unrest looms on the horizon at the novel's close—he is likewise unsuccessful in his attempt to realize through his mastery of the mine a perfected image of himself as powerful and self-sufficient, a foreordained outcome in a Lacanian reading. Having staked his identity on the success of the mine, the continuing instability in Sulaco that threatens his venture marks the precariousness of his sense of self. That is, if the independence of the mine is for Gould synonymous with a desired image of himself as autonomous, the narrative demonstrates that such hopes, both for the mine and for himself, are clearly delusive. This is a point made by Fogel, who speaks of Gould's "possessive identity," arguing that "he expresses, through the logic of his class, one of the main themes of the novel-that the means, such as 'property,' by which dependent people *must* seek to establish independence are themselves dependent, and can become illusions of self-sufficiency because all relation is in effect dependency."[16]

Certainly nowhere is the illusion of self-sufficiency produced by the embracing of an ideal more evident than in the relations of Gould to his fellow Costaguaneros. He is the silent Señor Administrador, the King of Sulaco, from whom the eager hide merchant Hirsch cannot extract a single "confirmatory word, a grunt of assent, a simple nod even."[17] Astride his horse, he moves in royal fashion among the people, condescending to reveal his thoughts only as necessary to ensure the safety of the mine, as in his dealings with Holroyd or in his involvement in Ribierist politics. Kiernan Ryan argues that in *Nostromo* "there is no real *exchange* either of language or experience." And surely Gould is the primary example of this "pervasive sense of stasis, of almost lifeless reification."[18] It is this silent withdrawal into himself—Martin Price describes him as living "within a fortress of polite silence"[19]—that destroys his marriage, leaving his wife to suffer a sterile, isolated existence; Gould, the narrator of Nostromo tells us, "seemed to dwell alone within a circumvallation of precious metal."[20]

Like Gould, Dr. Monygham defines himself by means of an ideal image. Yet whereas Gould seems to come to only a momentary awareness of his self-deception, as is suggested by his intimations of the "cruel futility of things"[21] as he observes the human wreckage of the revolution, the cynical doctor of Sulaco seems free of all illusions. Having betrayed his friends during the rule of tyrant Guzman Bento, he is consumed by an overwhelming sense of his own utter worthlessness. The memory of his extorted confession proves to him that he has made "truth, honour, self-respect, and life itself matters of little moment."[22] Still, in a way Monygham suffers from a delusion as powerful as that which grips Gould. The battered physician, the narrator informs us, has made for himself an "ideal conception of his disgrace."[23] He has become a "slave" to the memory of his betrayal.[24]

In convincing himself that he is perfect—perfect in disrepute—he embraces an identity as fixed and unreal as the personality Gould adopts as the powerful lord of the San Tomé mine. For Monygham is plainly not the arch-evil character he makes himself out to be; whatever his past failings, his conduct in the present belies the wicked self-image he has constructed for himself. In executing his duties as a physician, caring for the dying Teresa Viola as well those wounded in the revolutionary unrest, he shows himself to be a man of genuine compassion. Stephen K. Land describes him as a "dedicated humanitarian, deeply sensitive to the sufferings and misfortunes of others."[25] Nonetheless, believing in his own lack of worth as an individual, he lives his life for the most part in a self-imposed isolation from society; the crippled and scarred Señor Doctor becomes an outcast largely by his own choice.

If in the Lacanian view of human identity, the assumption of an ideal—a perfected conception of some sort—inevitably leads to alienation because the ideal is always illusory, the isolated lives of Gould and Monygham can be seen as testifying to what Lacan saw as a tragic fact of human existence. Although their conceptions of themselves are widely divergent, each creates an artificial personality, a notion of self that is unreal—a delusion. Like Gould, the "bitterly taciturn" Monygham attempts to realize his identity through something external to himself, in his case the neglected wife Emilia Gould, whom he decides to serve, he tells her, "to the whole extent of my evil reputation."[26] In a sense he uses her as a means of defining his own nothingness; he willingly risks his life to protect her, giving Sotillo false information about the whereabouts of the missing silver, but his impulse to self-sacrifice is premised upon an exaggerated notion of his own worthlessness. His successful deception of the revolutionaries, so crucial to the outcome of affairs in Sulaco, grows out of his obsession with his own disgrace: "He had said to himself bitterly, 'I am the only one fit for that dirty work.' And he believed this."[27] Thus, his fanatical commitment to Doña Emilia is strong evidence of the powerful "spirit of abasement" that we are told grips his life. By idealizing her—he believed her "worthy of every devotion"[28]—he is able to preserve his own negative ideal of himself. It is this fact, perhaps, that prompts Price to comment that Monygham's loyalty to Mrs. Gould is "as ruthless as any of the illusions we see in the novel."[29]

Certainly not without illusions is Nostromo himself, the magnificent Capataz de Cargadores, who for the Europeans of

Costaguana is the very embodiment of competence and reliability, for the native Costaguaneros a charismatic leader, a man of the people. In comparison to Gould and Monygham, his case seems fairly simple: he exists for no other reason than to be well spoken of—to nurture the "perfect form of his egoism."[30] Thus he, too, is undeniably an apt example of the Lacanian man fated to live outside himself, for it is only through the esteem and praise of his fellows that he is able to maintain a sense of identity; he has no conception whatever of a private self.

This complete displacement of identity—from a locus within the individual character and personality to the exterior judgments of others—accounts for the curious multiplying of names referring to Nostromo one finds in the novel: he is known variously as Nostromo, Capataz, Gian Battista, Juan, Giovanni, and Captain Fidanza. In a way, then, the "Other" he embraces is the whole of Costaguana, from the European émigrés to the Sulacan mozos and morenitas, in whose admiring eyes he has become a figure of unquestioned strength and courage. Underscoring the strictly public nature of Nostromo's identity is the fact that he is present in the first half of the novel virtually in name only. We meet the reputation rather than the man, yet we soon learn, in Nostromo's case the reputation is the man, a fact not lost on companion Martin Decoud: "It is curious to have met a man for whom the value of life seems to consist in personal prestige."[31]

The affair of the silver, in which Nostromo is the central agent, is crucial, therefore, not just in the defeating of Pedro Montero and the forces of federation, but in the undoing of the title character's idealized self-conception. Resolved that the spiriting away of the treasure is "the most desperate affair" of his life, Nostromo sees his successful completion of the dangerous task given to him as a means of confirming his image as it exists in the popular mind. "They shall learn I am just the man they take me for," he tells Decoud.[32] When his mission is thwarted by the collision of the lighter with the troopship from Esmeralda and the mysterious disappearance of four silver ingots in the suicide of Decoud, Nostromo is placed in a difficult position, for revealing the truth, he believes, might destroy the reputation he has so carefully nurtured. Ironically, however, in letting stand the belief that the treasure has gone to the bottom of the gulf—a notion he thinks will keep his public image intact—Nostromo unwittingly brings about the crisis in identity he had sought to avoid, for in the nonchalance with which the Europeans accept the news of the loss of the silver he sees that he is not held in as high esteem as he had previously thought, for his life has been risked needlessly. As one critic observes, "His sense of the meaning of his own identity is completely baffled, for it has been undervalued by the men to whom he was faithful."[33]

What Nostromo experiences is the death of his ideal, and, significantly, it is death that confronts him upon his return to Sulaco, in the hanging body of the tortured Hirsch and the shrouded corpse of Teresa Viola. The only thing truly lost in "that desperate affair," the narrator notes, was "his personality."[34] The text further records that after the hiding of the silver, "[Nostromo's] life seemed to fail him in all its details."[35] To Monygham, unexpectedly encountered at the deserted Custom House, he declares vehemently, "The Capataz is undone, destroyed. There is no Capataz. Oh, no! You will find the Capataz no more."[36] The self-important Captain Mitchell, describing his first meeting with Nostromo, after the removal of the silver, says, "At once I could see he was another man."[37] Possessing no clear sense of a private self, and no longer believing in the public image he had cultivated— everything was now "a sham"[38]—he becomes an empty, ineffectual figure; once the protector of the treasure, he becomes a thief. His inability to function as a private man is effectively demonstrated in his bumbling courtship of the Viola daughters, an episode sometimes criticized for lacking the intensity and interest of the earlier chapters, but in a way this "falling off" is precisely the point. Perhaps *Nostromo*'s close is superficial simply because that is what its title character has become.

There remains to be considered the important character Martin Decoud, Nostromo's companion on the fateful voyage of the lighter, forced to flee Sulaco when Monterist forces close in on the city. In a Lacanian reading of the text, which examines the ways in which characters appropriate objects external to themselves in an effort to realize an ideal identity, Decoud takes on significance in that he is manifestly unidealistic. Unlike Gould, Monygham, and Nostromo, he does not commit himself fully to anything. He remains throughout the work a thoroughly paradoxical figure: editor of the local Ribierist newspaper yet deeply distrustful of all political journalism, father of the newly formed Occidental Republic yet fully convinced of the foolishness of its leaders. He is both a Parisian dilettante and dandy recently arrived from Europe and a Spanish creole gentleman with a Costaguaneran heritage. There is, remarks C. B. Cox, "an element of pose in all the roles he assumes," a self-consciousness that "prevents him from ever achieving a fixed identity, for he cannot 'idealize' any one kind of purposeful action."[39] He falls in love, of course, with beautiful Antonia Avellanos, daughter of the famous Don José, but his profound scepticism creates what proves to be an insurmountable barrier between them, for he cannot devote himself unreservedly to the liberal patriotism both she and her father hold dear. He is a man, the narrator observes, "with no faith in anything except the truth of his own sensations,"[40] one for whom "the narrowness of every belief is odious."[41]

For Lacan the assumption of an ideal, albeit illusory, is a necessary step to functioning as an individual in the human community, to becoming a part of what he termed the symbolic order of language. Without the rigid armor of an identity, there is only fragmentation and disorder. In commenting upon his own mirror stage theory he once remarked, "This illusion of unity, in which a human being is always looking forward to self mastery, entails a constant danger of sliding back into the chaos from which he started; it hangs over the abyss of a dizzy Ascent in which one can perhaps see the very essence of Anxiety."[42] In the words of Catherine Clément, "the armor we wear is protection against madness"; to shed it—that is, to embrace no idealized conception of oneself in defining identity—"is to pass to the other side of a delicate curtain, to take the plunge and choose to communicate no more."[43]

It is in the light of these ideas that it is especially interesting to consider the death of Decoud, who takes, of course, a literal plunge into the gulf after shooting himself with a revolver and is "swallowed up into the immense indifference of things."[44] His fate can be seen as the inevitable outcome of his disavowal of all ideals; with no fixed sense of identity he can maintain no conception of the meaning of life, no hold on himself as a distinct entity. His individuality "had merged," the text records, "into the world of cloud and water, of natural forces and forms of nature."[45] Alone on the Great Isabel, cut off from all human contact, he is absorbed into a world of silence, the end for a man who "believed in nothing."[46]

The value of Lacan's ideas about the nature of identity formation lies in the fact that they help show that *Nostromo* is not so broad in its ambitions to explore the issues of society and history that it neglects altogether the workings of the individual mind. The characterizations of Charles Gould, Dr. Monygham, Nostromo, and Martin Decoud, when approached from a Lacanian perspective, evidence the text's concern with human psychology. *Nostromo* may very well be Conrad's "largest canvas," but it is surely one in which the artist does not overlook the "small details" of mental experience.

Notes

Editor's Note: opposite page 288, *Joseph Conrad*, by Dug Weston. Commissioned by *ELT*.

1. F. R. Leavis, *The Great Tradition* (New York: New York University Press, 1964), 196.

2. Ibid., 196–97.

3. Robert Penn Warren, 'The Great Mirage': Conrad and 'Nostromo'," *Selected Essays* (New York: Random House, 1958), 48.

4. Jacques Lacan, *Ecrits: A Selection*, Alan Sheridan, trans. (New York: Norton, 1977), 2.

5. Anika Lemaire, *Jacques Lacan* (London: Routledge, 1977), 176,

6. Aaron Fogel, *Coercion to Speak: Conrad's Poetics of Dialogue* (Cambridge: Harvard University Press, 1985), 114.

7. Joseph Conrad, *Nostromo* (1904; New York: Doubleday Page, 1916), 66.

8. Ibid., 82.

9. Ibid., 85

10. Joseph Wiesenfarth, *Gothic Manners and the Classic English Novel* (Madison: University of Wisconsin Press, 1988), 138.

11. *Nostromo*, 365.

12. Ibid., 65.

13. Ibid., 66.

14. Ibid., 245.

15. Dorothy Van Ghent, "Guardianship of the Treasure," in *Joseph Conrad: A Collection of Criticism*, Frederick Karl, ed. (New York: McGraw-Hill, 1975), 30.

16. Fogel, 115.

17. *Nostromo*, 201.

18. Kiernan Ryan, "Revelation and Repression in Conrad's Nostromo," *The Uses of Fiction: Essays on the Modern Novel in Honour of*

Arnold Kettle, Douglas Jefferson and Graham Martin, eds. (Milton Keynes: Open University Press, 1982), 79.

19. Martin Price, *Forms of Life: Character and Moral Imagination in the Novel* (New Haven: Yale University Press, 1983), 269.

20. *Nostromo*, 222.

21. Ibid., 364.

22. Ibid., 373.

23. Ibid., 375.

24. Ibid., 374.

25. Stephen K. Land, *Conrad and the Paradox of Plot* (London: Macmillan, 1984), 125.

26. *Nostromo*, 410.

27. Ibid., 439.

28. Ibid., 376.

29. Price, 260.

30. *Nostromo*, 301.

31. Ibid., 248.

32. Ibid., 267.

33. Van Ghent, 48.

34. *Nostromo*, 434.

35. Ibid., 422.

36. Ibid., 436.

37. Ibid., 488.

38. Ibid., 524.

39. C. B. Cox, *Joseph Conrad: The Modern Imagination* (London: J. M. Dent & Sons, 1974), 76.

40. *Nostromo*, 229.

41. Ibid., 187.

42. Quoted in Jane Gallop, *Reading Lacan* (Ithaca: Cornell University Press, 1995), 84.

43. Catherine Clément, *The Lives and Legends of Jacques Lacan* (New York: Columbia University Press, 1983), 91.

44. *Nostromo*, 501.

45. Ibid., 497.

46. Ibid., 500.

TRACY SEELEY

Conrad's Modernist Romance:
Lord Jim

Our best hopes are irrealisable; ... it is the almost incredible
misfortune of mankind, but also its highest privilege, to aspire
towards the impossible.

—Notes on Life and Letters

Vague terms like "modernism" can still signify, Michael Levenson notes
in beginning *The Genealogy of Modernism*; and in Conrad's case, the term
has by consensus been remarkably specific.[1] Studies of his modernism
inevitably invoke the isolation of consciousness, the indeterminacy of
language and experience, philosophical skepticism and literary
innovation. Considered by at least one critic the modernist novel's
inaugural text, *Lord Jim*'s publication on the emblematic century mark
has only heightened its literary historical importance.[2] While recent
revisions of modernism should make us wary of viewing either Conrad
or *Lord Jim* as modernism's paradigm, the novel's disrupted chronology,
subjective narrators, and thematic indeterminacy place *Lord Jim* securely
among the modernists.[3]

Yet the criticism that has proliferated around the modernist
Conrad has uneasily accommodated that "other" Conrad: the
nineteenth-century Polish romantic, the morally certain teller of
popular tales. In part, the writer's own self-contradiction lies at the root

Seeley, Tracy. "Conrad's Modernist Romance: *Lord Jim*." *ELH* 59 (1992): 495–511. © 1992
by The Johns Hopkins University Press. Reprinted by permission of The Johns Hopkins
University Press.

of our divided critical attention. What Albert J. Guerard saw in 1958 as
a conflict between "cosmic skepticism and extreme commitment to
order" still shapes current criticism.[4] Levenson elaborates on the
analogous tension, for example, in the Preface to "The Nigger of the
'Narcissus,'" where he sees Conrad defining the artist's two tasks: in
one, the artist who values the unconscious "steadfastness of Old
Singleton" will "make [us] see"; and in the other, the artist who values
the narrator's consciousness will "descend within himself."[5]
Unconscious diligence as an absolute value, and the subjective
consciousness as the arbiter of value. So we have seen two Conrads in
part because he has seemed of two minds. He can lament, as he does in
Outcast of the Islands, "the tremendous fact of our isolation, of the
loneliness impenetrable and transparent, elusive and everlasting" (250),
and speak with equal conviction about the "Community of Mankind."
Or he can write that the universe is an indifferent knitting machine
unaffected by human wishes that it occasionally embroiders, while
celebrating Solidarity, Fidelity or Duty, those few simple ideas on which
the world rests.[6] The world rests on solid ground; the world rests on
nothingness. This is the Conrad we know well: his trademark idealism
and skepticism locked in familiar tension.

But in part, criticism has perhaps too readily acceded to the
modernists' sense of apocalypse and radical departure from the past, as
Perry Meisel argues.[7] Equating Conrad's modernism with fin-de-siècle
skepticism and its aesthetic effects has exacerbated our sense of his
contradictions. In effect, Conrad's modern moment marks the
confluence of many streams: aesthetic, historical, political,
philosophical, personal—not all of them amenable to received notions of
what counts as modernist. Together, these causes have especially
hampered reconciling Conrad's modernist thought and aesthetics with
his tenacious loyalty to the forms of romance. In comparing *Arrow of
Gold*, for example, to *The Secret Agent* or *Under Western Eyes*, no
reconciliation is called for. Critics can rightly bracket the Conrad least
relevant to the work at hand, pointing either to the writer's inconsistency
or to his evolutionary development. But for *Lord Jim* especially, we must
attend to both Conrads at once; for here, more dramatically than in any
other work, his contradictions inform a single text. And our difficulties
start with "A Romance," Conrad's own subtitle for the novel.[8]

To both Conrad and his audience, "romance" suggested the
exploits of an exemplary protagonist—who, after heroic difficulty, reaps

enviable and predictable rewards: fame, glory, retribution, wealth or power—perhaps all of the above. Conrad's Jim, the novel's ostensible focus, clearly meets such popular expectations. Faced with the novel's narrative and epistemological complexity, though, those who embrace its literariness usually tend to minimize the subtitle by relegating it to the Patusan episode; point to its incongruity beside his impressionism; or replace it with others—modernist, writerly, self-reflexive.[9] All fit. I would like to suggest, however, that "A Romance" describes the whole of *Lord Jim*, and not simply its tale of a hapless adventurer far from home, an unself-conscious romantic who wanders into that most exotic locale, a modernist novel. Here, I return to the quotation at the top of this essay, to suggest a connection between the generic designation "Romance" and Conrad's modernism, a link suggested by his observation that it is both high tragedy and inestimable privilege for mankind to aspire to the impossible.

As we know, romance from its medieval beginnings has been about aspirations to the ideal: quests for the Grail, heroism, the perfect lover, the ideal society—the search for happy endings. Modernist skepticism clearly militates against happy endings; but romance does not simply disappear in the twentieth century, or thrive only in the publishing industry's pulp mills. Instead, one branch begins self-consciously to recognize and attend to the impossibility of its own ideal aims. To borrow Harold Bloom's term, this "gnostic or demonic romance" "unwillingly exposes the goal as delusive" and yet "values the journey more than the destination, and leaves us something other than a sense of loss."[10] It seems clear that *Lord Jim* is such a romance, exploring human aspiration not simply to the ideal, but to the admittedly impossible. It examines and insists on the delusiveness of ideals, and on recognizing the delusion, and yet it also promotes those ideals as both important and necessary. Thus Conrad's modernist self-consciousness and skepticism, his epistemological doubt and attention to the inadequacies of language, do not overwhelm or shunt aside, debate or alternate with his romance.[11] The two are inseparable. In *Lord Jim*, the crises that many modernists perceived to be their lot converge on the idealist's vision, and modernist romance emerges. In fact, it takes on a variety of guises, as the opposing impulses of dream and disillusion shape three romance narratives: Jim's, Marlow's and Conrad's. Each narrator aspires to an ideal, and in narrating exposes the limits of his own gnostic perception.

Ultimately for Conrad, the most compelling romance also most fully admits the limits of its aims.

The first romance, Jim's failed quest for ideal selfhood, even more clearly articulates his failure to acknowledge his goal's impossibility. That failure prevents him from achieving the selfhood that gnostic self-fashioning makes possible. Marlow's self-understanding, on the other hand, includes the skepticism wrought by failure and finds that failure mediated by a community of others like him. This understanding both gives rise to and contravenes the novel's second romance: the quest to redeem Jim through narrative, thereby maintaining Marlow's community and the stability of meaning it affords. In that quest, Marlow reaches his own limits of understanding, blind to the dangers of the political romance he constructs for Jim. And finally, Conrad's quest for unambiguous closure, mirrored in Marlow's search for understanding, becomes *Lord Jim*'s third romance.

In all three narratives, recognizing impossibility matters as much to Conrad as the ideals themselves. And in every case, necessary disillusionment is mediated by community, that ideal organic entity that becomes a last defense against nihilism and isolation.[12] While for Conrad, skepticism has eroded possibilities for absolute truth and certain knowledge, community creates the ground of consensual understanding. In community, Conrad can yet hope for meaningful identity and action, and for storytelling that is more than textuality alone. Yet even that communal ideal becomes subject to the knowing disillusionment of gnostic romance. How Conrad avoids despair on this count, we shall see.

I: Jim's Romance of Integrity

For critics, Marlow's unreliability has long since stolen the spotlight from questions of Jim's "nature" or the puzzle of either betrayal or triumph on Patusan. As Fredric Jameson and others have noted, *Lord Jim*'s real "event" is Marlow's "analysis and dissolution of" Jim's fortunes.[13] We know little more of Jim than Marlow hears or thinks to tell us; and so we struggle with obfuscation and misdirection, with a narrator whose own motives and aspirations bear watching. Yet for Conrad, something besides Marlow's account is at stake in Jim's drama of personal integrity, played in the gap between idealized self-perception and recognized imperfection. Jim's figure and the pilgrim ship story that inspired the novel seem to have appealed to the writer's characteristic fascination with this theme. So if we can, for a moment, naively consider Jim's character, we come close to the heart of Conrad's own skeptical negotiation with the Ideal.

Conrad's fascination with self-idealizing and the shock of recognizing an embodied "other" self appears repeatedly: in the doppleganger of "The Secret Sharer," for example, or in more subtle pairings like Marlow and Kurtz. Wanting his real and ideal selves to be identical, Jim hopes to achieve absolute and static identity, an undivided and transcendently perfect self. This becomes his utopian romance goal. But integrity in Conrad entails integrating both selves, not abandoning or denying the "darker" self.[14] Idealization and gnostic recognition together make a coherent self possible, protected from nihilism and the extinction of self-identity. Cox observes that in *Nostromo*, for example, an ideal self-conception "keeps the ghost-world at bay," by constructing a stable self resistant to futility and meaningless. Thus Decoud, with no such ideal, succumbs to suicidal despair; and Nostromo, whose self-identity rests solely on his reputation among others, finds ultimately that he is no one.[15] Jim's ego-ideal may thus protect him from despair; but for Conrad, that ideal must be countered by admitting its illusory nature. This admission, which distinguishes "gnostic" from "popular" romance, also clarifies, by contrast, Jim's peculiar form of romanticism.

Stein's calling Jim "romantic" has rarely been opposed; it seems aptly to describe the idealistic seaman, his boyhood reading and heroic dreams. In fact, his dreams come through the pages of popular romance, and in this mediated sense, Jim is romantic, as Don Quixote is romantic. Admiring his goals and lamenting his failure, we can wink slyly to one another and call his naivete, of course, romantic. Or we can call his overly-active imagination "romantic"—a sort of creative over-abundance. As we know, Conrad often warned against this very temptation to excess. In Tony Tanner's words, for Conrad "it causes the mind to slide away from the 'saving facts' of life and indulge in immobilising fantasies of terror or glory."[16] We see this feared effect aboard the training ship, just prior to Jim's first maritime crisis. Below decks, Jim imagines

> saving people from sinking ships, cutting away masts in a hurricane.... He confronted savages on tropical shores,

quelled mutinies on the high seas, and in a small boat upon
the ocean kept up the hearts of despairing men—always an
example of devotion to duty, and as unflinching as a hero in
a book. (6)

Shortly after, transfixed by these visions and the force of the storm, Jim
can't integrate dreams and reality, and he fails to perform any of his
imagined roles. The same dissonance aboard the *Patna* virtually
guarantees his "accident." Early in the voyage, Jim stands mesmerized
on deck, "his eyes, roaming about the line of the horizon, seemed to gaze
hungrily into the unattainable, and did not see the shadow of the coming
event" (19). In fact he sees something quite different: an imagined crisis
too terrifying to confront. Imaginatively transforming the sleeping
pilgrims, Jim stands

> surveying the silent company of the dead. They *were* dead!
> Nothing could save them! There were boats enough for half
> of them perhaps, but there was no time. No time! No time!
> ... There was no help. He imagined what would happen
> perfectly. (86)

As the narrator has already told us, this is "Imagination, the enemy of
men, the father of all terrors" (11). Blinded by dreams, Jim cannot act.
And for Conrad, this failure has social implications beyond the
abandonment of pilgrims. The excessive inward romantic gaze, the
transformative imagination unweighted by realistic perception, and the
self-aggrandizing model of achievement, together keep Jim from
meeting his ideal's first requirement: "devotion to duty."

In fact, Jim's first great leap from the life he has sworn to uphold
comes not in abandoning the *Patna*, but in boarding it. That action's
inspiration is especially revealing. Waiting to recover from his back
injury and return to England, Jim at first disdains the other men
lingering about the Eastern port. They hardly comport with his
standards:

> They had now a horror of the home service, with its harder
> conditions, severer view of duty, and the hazard of stormy
> oceans. They were attuned to the eternal peace of Eastern

sky and sea. They loved short passages, good deck-chairs, large native crews, and the distinction of being white. (13)

But gradually, Jim's evaluation changes:

> At length he found a fascination in the sight of those men, in their appearance of doing so well on such a small allowance of danger and toil. In time, beside the original disdain there grew up slowly another sentiment; and suddenly, giving up the idea of going home, he took a berth as chief mate of the *Patna*. (13)

Neither Jim's decision nor its suddenness comes as a surprise. As we already know, the life of duty has proven uncongenial with his imagined version of it; since first following the siren song of the maritime,

> he had [had] to bear the criticism of men, the exactions of the sea, and the prosaic severity of the daily task that gives bread—but whose only reward is in the perfect love of the work. This reward eluded him. (10)

Jim's glamorous self-perception and idealization of sea life contain no room for criticism, exactions, and severity—particularly the prosaic kind. The very notion of *eluding* duty appeals to him, and when the *Patna* presents an escape, he leaps at the chance.

No wonder, then, that repeatedly in crisis, Jim stands alone, isolated from the claims of solidarity. Even his confession, usually an acceptance of responsibility, ascribes the blame to others:

> Oh, yes, I know very well—I jumped. I told you I jumped; but I tell you.... It was their doing as plainly as if they had reached up with a boat hook and pulled me over. Can't you see it? You must see it. Come. (123)

Superior to culpability and to the *Patna* crew, "those men [who] did not belong to the world of heroic adventure" (24), Jim naturally feels little empathy for his "cargo." Even after knowing some measure of communal responsibility on Patusan, Jim still feels as though "nothing can touch me" (325). And few things *can* touch him, protected as he is from human claims in his bastion of imagined privilege.

So in its pejorative senses, applied to popular fiction, overwrought imagination, the separation of heroes from the rest of us—"romantic" will do. But that sense is not Conrad's, at least not in this novel. Jim's romance lacks gnosis, the knowing that informs a different understanding of desire and disillusionment. In this conception, which Marlow, Stein and Conrad share, Jim never achieves full romantic status. Integrity eludes him. For while imagined ideals always inscribe the disparity between wish and fulfillment, Jim never understands this; he never consciously incorporates his deals into a narrative of self-understanding that includes his failure to achieve them. That narrative is fundamental to Marlow's self-understanding, and to the fellowship of the craft.

II: Marlow's More Knowing Romance

Jim's interlocutor immediately recognizes the distance between Jim's desires and the world, a disjunction endemic to a life at sea:

> In no other kind of life is the illusion more wide of reality—
> in no other is the beginning *all* illusion—the disenchantment
> more swift—the subjugation more complete. Hadn't we all
> commenced with the same desire, ended with the same
> knowledge, carried the memory of the same cherished
> glamour through the sordid days of imprecation? (129)

Like a beacon, the memory of those ideals illuminates the landscape and guides the fellowship; but it clearly mustn't be confused with the terrain itself. Instead, the gnostic imagination weaves desire, knowledge and memory into a narrative of identity. Jim's memory of the *Patna* ought to become part of a similar story, but he never recognizes his ideals' necessary entanglement in failure. Thus he does not construct his own narrative of loss, which would solidify his belonging in the fellowship. For that community depends not only on its code of conduct, but on this common story of disillusionment. Repeatedly, as if to reinforce the fellowship, Marlow appeals to his audience's memory of their own brief "light of glamour" and disenchantment; the "events of the sea" had revealed "the secret truth of [their] pretences both to others and to themselves" (10). Ideals and disillusionment together sustain their community, which Jim will not join. Even Marlow, bent on making Jim "one of us," notes his subject's failure here: the competing realms of dreams and duty remain intractably separate. By not knowing what to do with his disillusionments, or even acknowledging them, Jim remains an outsider.

Writing "Youth" virtually alongside *Heart of Darkness* and *Lord Jim*, Conrad heard that story "sounding the note" for a "moral idea" common to all three works.[17] Among several common notes, we hear this resounding interest in dreams like Jim's, in integrating and valuing the loss entailed in maturation. In "Youth," Marlow reminisces about his own idealistic and self-important youth, his imprudent dreams abandoned to memory, just as in *Lord Jim*. The same theme would also inform *The Shadow-Line*. Reflecting on youth and age in that story, Cox characterizes the shadow-line not as a "clear dividing place ... but that transitional period when we abandon the illusory dreams of youth, and settle down to cope with our own mediocrity."[18] The *Patna* should have been Jim's shadow-line, but he learns nothing. As Marlow remarks, Jim "had no leisure to regret what he had lost, he was so wholly and naturally concerned for what he had failed to obtain" (83). And so Jim lives in unending and static anticipation, always ready for glorious achievement just around the corner. Failure brings neither self-understanding nor commitment to others. Instead he confesses, "what a chance missed! My God! what a chance missed!" (83). This opportunism persists even as Jim arrives in Patusan and embraces his new, "magnificent chance" (241).

Eyes still fixed on glamor in this land of new opportunity, Jim hasn't mastered Marlow's trick of living in both realms—of dreaming and waking—at the same time. For all the baffling logic of Stein's famous metaphor, Conrad surely had this in mind: that dreamers like Jim, whose reach exceeds their grasp, must learn to live in two worlds at once, as Conrad had.[19] Stein notes this "balance of colossal forces" in nature, its "perfect equilibrium" shaping his own history and self-understanding. Victory over assailants or a prized butterfly counterbalances the knowledge that dreams can, like the match he holds, go in an instant: "'Friend, wife, child,' he said, slowly, gazing at the small flame—'phoo!' The match was blown out" (211). Unlike Stein, Jim lacks this equilibrium; he doesn't understand that his envisioned self, "a very fine fellow," is one "so fine as he can never be" (213). Calling both Jim and Stein "romantic" equivocates on this fundamental difference. Clearly, Jim is not "one of us."

So what is Jim, after all? Answers to that question occupy volumes, as critics try to uncover Conrad's intentions or solve Marlow's final riddle. But surely Jim's failure to account for his "jump" in less than opportunistic terms, to embrace the gap between dreams and the world, or to achieve integrity all prohibit his playing "tragic hero," as early critics cast him.[20] Jim's response to Gentleman Brown, in fact, seems conditioned foremost by his habitual naivete, and his unacknowledged complicity with mankind. So Jim may feel accused by Brown, but is certainly not affronted by a mirror of his own imperfection.

Ultimately, though, does this make Jim wholly accountable for Cornelius's treachery and Brown's atrocities? To say so requires Jim's own moral simplicity, as well as his habit of organizing the universe around himself. But to construct a causal chain implicating only Jim is a seductive and interesting temptation, and one whose implications further distinguish Jim's romance from Conrad's. As we've seen, Jim's idealization, unfettered by disillusionment and the shared narrative of loss, confounds both collective identity and individual integrity. This Marlow clearly understands. Yet elevating Jim to a privileged status at the center of the text—either a hero who dies for honor or fool who dies for nothing—is itself an idealizing movement into which Marlow lures the reader.[21]

Compelled to maintain his faith in solidarity and its "fixed standard of conduct," Marlow cannot abandon his subject. But such fixity masks an inconsistency in his reading of Jim, a confusion between Jim's failure and a possible failure of the code of conduct. As a shared ideal that cements community, the code's perfection yet remains elusive, both aim and human failing locked in the romance dialectic that Marlow has repeatedly acknowledged. Yet he often ignores or forgets this when it comes to Jim. Although Jim hasn't allowed "Fidelity" to mediate the isolation of his imagined heroism, Marlow persistently describes him as "one of us," that is, one who lives by the code. Why the confusion? Or the fascination with Jim's commonplace failing? Why the pains to ameliorate it in the narrative? Marlow also wonders:

> Why I longed to go grubbing into the deplorable details of
> an occurrence which, after all, concerned me no more than

as a member of an obscure body of men held together by a
community of inglorious toil and by fidelity to a certain
standard of conduct, I can't explain. (50)

But of course, it's a self-answering riddle; Marlow's identity rests with
that "obscure body"—and he needs to make certain of it. Jim's threat to
that certainty keeps Marlow riveted not simply on an enigma, but on an
adversary, a foe to his own remembered youth and the community which
shares it. So Marlow averts the danger by deemphasizing and delaying
the "facts" of the case and in effect, idealizing the protagonist.[22] By
making Jim "one of us," Marlow maintains a coherent "us" and thus a
coherent sense of himself. But in the process, he abandons his
gnosticism, failing to see the far-reaching political dangers of his own
self-protective idealism. By contrast, Conrad maintains his own
gnosticism well beyond the limits of the fellowship's embracing
assurances. By first redefining true community and the grounds for
certainty, he shows those ideals to be what they have always been:
conventional illusions, whose force is nonetheless undiminished. And
then, he turns from heroism toward the virtues that make community—
both author and beneficiary of those conventions—viable.

Kenneth Bruffee's illuminating study, *Elegiac Romance*, describes
Lord Jim as the story of yet another disillusionment: Marlow's coming to
terms with modern culture's loss of the hero. As the narrator of elegiac
romance, Bruffee argues, Marlow "saturate[s] his description of his hero
with his own personality, his own values, and above all his own deepest
emotional problems." This sympathy ultimately frees the narrator from
hero-worship—and in its place formulates "an exemplary virtue
adequate to modern life as he perceived it."[23] I would argue rather that
Marlow's ambivalence and conflicting narrative intentions indicate a
lingering tendency toward hero-worship. Nonetheless, Bruffee rightly
suggests that through Marlow, Conrad challenges the formulaic heroism
to which Jim aspires, and

dissects an important element of Western culture, the ethos
of masculinity founded on a belief in mastery—self-control,
control of the conditions of one's life, virtues that make one
superior, presumably, to those who lack this control. (94)

Jim clearly aspires to these ideals, which Jameson claims also underpin Conrad's romance more generally.[24] Popular romance, he argues, necessarily entails an ideology of domination based on an "ethics of binary opposition." That is, those cultures designated not "us," but "other" are "repudiated and marginalized in practices which are then ultimately themselves formalized in the concept of evil."[25] In this view, Conrad's opposition to colonial abuses, for example, does not mitigate the ethics embodied in romance; nor does Conrad seem aware of the blindspots in his own critiques. Nevertheless, his advocacy of a gnostic romance distinct from the moral simplicity of Jim's romance suggests a more complex understanding than Jameson claims.[26] Jim's dreams of mastery promise a political organization based on the domination of "others" by "one of us"; while for Conrad, individual integrity and collective identity both depend on a different ethos. He often hints at this difference. For example, in the "Author's Note" to *Almayer's Folly*, Conrad took a letter-writer to task for calling his fiction "uncivilized." Conrad assumed that the epithet specifically described "the strange people and far-off countries" embodied in his work. But his critic's judgment, Conrad answered, "has nothing to do with justice.... [There] is a bond between us and that humanity so far away. I am content to sympathize with common mortals, no matter where they live."[27] Conrad's "fidelity" extends beyond the white British "ranks" implied by Marlow's "us," a definition betrayed when Jim's appearance proves deceptive. Failing to understand the implications of his surprise, Marlow recalls that he "would have trusted" that "clean-limbed, clean-faced" boy who seems "one of us"; and "it wouldn't have been safe" (40, 45). To Marlow, the danger remains anomalous, a puzzle; but his last reader exposes the ethics implicit in Marlow's concept of "us." Marlow writes:

> You prophesied for [Jim] the disaster of weariness and of disgust with acquired honour.... You had said you knew so well 'that kind of thing,' its illusory satisfaction, its unavoidable deception.... [You claimed that] 'giving your life up to "them,"' (*them* meaning all of mankind with skins brown, yellow, or black in colour) 'was like selling your soul to a brute.' (338–39)

Marlow's apparent criticism here reveals his blindness; for he does not address the denigration of "otherness," suggesting instead that Jim participated in no social transaction all. His insistence, however, that "of all mankind Jim had no dealings but with himself" (339), hints by contrast at Conrad's own wider view of fidelity to "mankind." Conrad professed

> an impartial view of humanity in all its degrees of splendour and misery together with a special regard for the rights of the underprivileged of this earth, not on any mystic ground but on the ground of simple fellowship and honourable reciprocity of services. (*Personal Record*, ix)

As Avrom Fleishman has recently argued, Conrad, like Jameson, envisions the "transcendence of class in national unities, on the way toward international homogeneity."[28] Fleishman obviously delights in Jameson's invocation of Durkheim, who shares an organicist tradition with Conrad. Despite their obvious differences, though, both romances of collectivity—Marxist and Conradian—imply a reciprocity absent from Jim's benevolent dictatorship. Admittedly feeling changed once enmeshed in "the life of the people," he still feels responsible *for* and not *to* them. His heroic ideal and commitment to Jewel and her people are ultimately incompatible.

As Bruffee argues, then, Conrad redefined the heroic ethos in opposition to Jim's colonial rule—a distinction Marlow fails to see. And thus Marlow vacillates between wanting Jim to be one of us and alternately regretting and hoping that he is not, perhaps also because he recognizes the danger in his narrative impulse.[29] Critical studies that see Patusan only as a "never-never land" or as Conrad's recourse to popular literary modes might well examine these dangers.[30] For clearly, the novel's second half tests the implicit hypothesis of its first: that romance hopes vested in a single hero—either by himself or by others— necessarily fail, for both hero and hero-makers. For all the ostensible benefits Jim brings to Patusan, native faith in his "unfailingness" mirrors Jim's own deluded faith in achieving perfect selfhood. The natives have, in fact, made Jim the hero of his musings, "the visible, tangible incarnation of unfailing truth and of unfailing victory" (361).[31] But Jim and his loyalists share a blindness to the impossibility of their desires; Patusan's restored "belief in the stability of earthly institutions since the return of the white lord" (387) will be short-lived. For Conrad, political authority must be distributed amidst the "organic unity" of a "spiritual and cultural union" and sustained in other ways.[32]

Given this programme, however, Conrad never optimistically envisioned the achievement of such a union; like the novel's other ideals, his ideal community remains "a beckoning but evasive realm of higher possibility."[33] This desire for a necessary and admittedly impossible ideal has its correlate in the novel's third romance: the quest for closure. Clearly, Marlow's desire for understanding generates his tale, and just as clearly guarantees his frustration, a futility he also recognizes. Here Marlow's and Conrad's romances merge: both are storytellers who cannot present transcendent truth or convey unequivocal meaning. And yet in this final gnostic romance, Conrad's disillusionment again does not end in despair. Like community, the narrator's authority and possibilities for meaning must be redefined and sustained in other ways as well.

III: Conrad's Romance of Community and Closure

Marlow, intent on answering his final question, "Is he satisfied?," nonetheless recognizes the impossibility of knowing. He recalls that "the less I understood, the more I was bound to him in the name of that doubt which is the inseparable part of knowledge" (221). His knowledge inextricably bound to doubt, Marlow speaks as a modernist romance narrator, assessing the futility of his task: "Are not our lives too short for that full utterance which through all our stammerings is of course our only and abiding intention?" (225). And so, the final image "of that incomplete story [is] its incompleteness itself" (337); and the "meaning" of the story's facts rests somewhere amidst the haze of subjectivity. Isolated with his impressions and non-conclusions, *Lord Jim*'s narrator must depend on something other than faith in essential meaning. Confronted with this now-familiar epistemological quandary, Marlow turns to his listeners.

It has become a commonplace that creating community in the modern world becomes the artist's task; Bruffee extends this function to the narrator, who while telling his tale, creates a "community of sympathetic readers."[34] Thus the modernist narrator, beset by inadequate and inconclusive vision, might nonetheless escape solipsism through the very act of storytelling. In *A Personal Record*, Conrad suggests this possibility:

> What is a novel if not a conviction of our fellow-man's existence strong enough to take upon itself a form of imagined life clearer than reality and whose accumulated verisimilitude of selected episodes puts to shame the pride of documentary history? (15)

This conviction allows Conrad also to believe in a community of listeners or readers, which in effect creates a ground of belief in its assent to "see" what the narrator sets before them—temporarily dispelling the chaos of disparate perceptions. Community again becomes a mediating structure, the illusion of truth and certainty sustained by, and in turn sustaining, a community of like souls. Sharing Conrad's certainty that "my conviction gains infinitely the moment another soul will believe in it," Marlow tells his story; fear that, like Patusan, it would "slip out of existence" has "incited me to tell you the story, to try to hand over to you, as it were, its very existence, its reality—the truth disclosed in a moment of illusion" (323). An interpretive community forms in those hours of shared illusion, as artistic consciousness and commitment to others now sustains meaning, by dispersing the authority of the text among many. But as Bruffee fails to note, this aspiration to collective identity and authority is likewise bound to the disillusionment of gnostic romance.

More than once, Marlow regrets that the fellowship of the craft is less dependable than its ideal counterpart. And while interviewing Jim, Marlow, speaking like the skeptic Conrad, philosophizes that

> it is when we try to grapple with another man's intimate need that we perceive how incomprehensible, wavering and misty are the beings that share with us the sight of the stars and the warmth of the sun. It is as if loneliness were a hard and absolute condition of our existence. (179–80)

And of course, the moment Marlow's narrative ends, the illusion of an interpretive consensus vanishes. The story's incompleteness "made discussion vain and comment impossible" as "[each] of them seemed to carry away his own impression, to carry it away with him like a secret" (337). Fragmentation of both community and meaning constantly threaten in this modernist romance; but as long as the story continues, as it does first for the privileged reader and then for us, Conrad holds despair at bay. Chapters 37–45, where Marlow collects the story's last fragments to create the illusion of a coherent narrative, perpetuates the movement toward understanding. The final event, he says, "had to happen…. I've fitted the pieces together, and there is enough of them to make an intelligible picture" (343). The enticing possibility of a complete and coherent picture once again sets the quest for the transcendent—in this case, closure—in opposition to its acknowledged impossibility.

We, like the privileged reader, peruse these last fragments "like one approaching with slow feet and alert eyes the glimpse of an undiscovered country." The horizon of a full account and absolute closure beckons; even when we, like Marlow's reader, have forsworn the romance hopes of ever arriving in the "ever-undiscovered country over the hill, across the stream, beyond the wave" (338). In *Lord Jim*, finally, there is neither transcendence nor despair. For the novel's final questions extend the search for order indefinitely and leave us with this ever-unresolved tension. Conrad, however, values this inconclusiveness and the determination, as in a true romance, to go on regardless. In an excised passage from the preface to "The Nigger of the 'Narcissus,'" he writes that "the consciousness of a worthy aim is everything; it is conscience, dignity, truth, honour—the reward and the peace."[35] Knowing that the aim is futile, that hallmark knowledge of modernist romance, creates a new romance ideal with the ability yet to bind us together in the ongoing search for meaning. The author's letter to the *New York Times* (1901), describes this ideal:

> The only legitimate basis of creative work lies in the courageous recognition of all irreconcilable antagonisms that make our life so enigmatic, so burdensome, so fascinating, so dangerous—so full of hope…. [The] barren struggle of contradictions assumes the dignity of moral strife.[36]

The open-endedness, and unendingness, of that struggle guarantees the ongoing quest for meaning, closure and community. For it perpetuates Conrad's romance beyond the text, into the world of readers like us.[37]

NOTES

1. Michael Levenson, *The Genealogy of Modernism* (Cambridge: Cambridge Univ. Press, 1984), 1.

2. John Batchelor holds this view in *Lord Jim* (Winchester, Mass.: Unwin Human, 1988), 2. Joseph Warren Beach describes Conrad's "impressionism" in *The Twentieth Century Novel: Studies in Technique* (New York: Appleton–Century, 1932), 337-65; as does Cedric Watts in *The Deceptive Text* (Sussex: Harvester Press, 1984). Other studies focus on modernist epistemology and its literary effects. For example, see C. B. Cox, *Joseph Conrad: The Modern Imagination* (New Jersey: Rowman and Littlefield, 1974); Patrick Whiteley, *Knowledge and Experimental Realism* (Baton Rouge: Louisiana State Univ. Press, 1987). Studies of skepticism include *Conrad's Models of Mind* (Minneapolis: Univ. of Minnesota Press, 1971), in which Bruce Johnson traces Conrad's debt to Schopenhauer; Mark Wollaeger breaks new ground by more thoroughly delineating the philosophical skepticist tradition and its place in Conrad's work in *Joseph Conrad and the Fictions of Skepticism* (Stanford: Stanford Univ. Press, 1990).

3. Recent revisions generally address the degree to which the production, canonization and critical reception of these works are themselves implicated in early twentieth-century European culture. For example, Sandra M. Gilbert and Susan Gubar argue for a redefinition incorporating more women's texts and the sexual politics of the period; see *No Man's Land: The Place of the Woman Writer in the Twentieth Century* (New Haven: Yale Univ. Press, 1988), especially vol. 1. Shari Benstock argues for similar critical refocusing in *Women of the Left Bank* (Austin: Univ. of Texas Press, 1986). For a history of the modernist/realist debates begun by Lukacs in the 1930s, see Bruce Robbins, "Modernism in History, Modernism in Power," in *Modernism Reconsidered*, ed. Robert Kiely (Cambridge: Harvard Univ. Press, 1983), 147–66. In *The Myth of the Modern* (New Haven: Yale Univ. Press, 1986), Perry Meisel also attempts a cultural revision, arguing that criticism has blindly accepted the modernists' claims for a "primacy beyond culture" (232). But by positing a universal sense of belatedness to account for modernist aesthetic practices, Meisel erases the very culture he insists on restoring to discussion.

4. Albert J. Guerard, *Conrad the Novelist* (Cambridge: Harvard Univ. Press, 1958), 11.

5. Levenson (note 1), 1–22.

6. Paul Armstrong argues that trying to resolve this tension—and being unable to—comprises the "challenge of bewilderment" endemic to modernism; see *The Challenge of Bewilderment: Understanding and Representation in James, Conrad and Ford* (Ithaca: Cornell Univ. Press, 1987), part 2.

7. See note 3 above.

8. This subtitle appeared beginning with the First American Edition, published by Doubleday and McClure Co., 1900. My references here are to *Lord Jim: A Romance* (New York: Doubleday, Page and Co., 1924), with page numbers noted parenthetically in the text. References to other Conrad works are also to the 1924 Doubleday, Page editions, unless otherwise noted.

9. Fredric Jameson even claims the first part of *Lord Jim* for postmodernism, a paradigm of ecriture, a "breathtaking [exercise] in nonstop textual production"; see *The Political Unconscious: Narrative as a Socially Symbolic Act* (Ithaca: Cornell Univ. Press, 1981), 219. Ted Billy makes a similar argument in his Introduction to *Critical Essays on Joseph Conrad*, ed. Ted Billy (Boston, Mass.: G.K. Hall, 1987), 15.

10. Harold Bloom, *Ringers in the Tower: Studies in Romantic Tradition* (Chicago: Univ. of Chicago Press, 1971), 3. William Bonney calls Conrad's romance "disteleological," emphasizing the "adamant absence" of the transcendent order implied by romance questing; see *Thorns and Arabesques: Contexts for Conrad's Fiction* (Baltimore: Johns Hopkins Univ. Press, 1980). Conrad's insistent recognition of that absence, however, makes "gnostic romance" a more compelling description.

11. David Thorburn successfully integrates the two "halves" of Conrad's temperament by tracing both his modernist self-consciousness and "stoic" sense of "human sharing and continuity" to the Romantic tradition; see *Conrad's Romanticism* (New Haven: Yale Univ. Press, 1974), x, xi.

12. I am relying here on Avrom Fleishman's articulation of the organicist tradition in Conrad; see *Conrad's Politics: Community and Anarchy in the Fiction of Joseph Conrad* (Baltimore: Johns Hopkins Univ. Press, 1967). Subsequent challenges to Fleishman's account have not successfully displaced it. For a retrospective account of these challenges and Fleishman's response to them, see his "Reminiscing," *Conradiana* 19 (1987): 18–30.

13. Jameson (note 9), 257.

14. Steve Ressler sees integrity or the affirmation of self "at the heart of Conrad's moral preoccupations"; see *Joseph Conrad: Consciousness and Integrity* (New York: New York Univ. Press, 1988), 1. But integrity's cost is not, as he claims, the "renunciation of the world" (5). Affirmation of the self in Conrad's gnostic romance, depends on renouncing neither the ideal nor the world.

15. Cox (note 2), 54–64, 76.

16. Tony Tanner, *Conrad: Lord Jim*, Studies in English Literature 12 (London: E. Arnold, 1963), 29.

17. *Joseph Conrad's Letters to William Blackwood and David S. Meldrum*, ed. William Blackburn (Durham: Duke Univ. Press, 1958), 26 December 1899; 19 May 1900.

18. Cox (note 2), 150.

19. To recall Stein's oft-quoted parable: "Very funny this terrible thing is. A man that is born falls into a dream like a man who falls into the sea. If he tries to climb out into the air, as inexperienced people endeavour to do, he drowns.... No! I tell you! The way is to the destructive element submit yourself, and with the exertions of your hands and feet in the water make the deep, deep sea keep you up" (214). In other words, the dream can sustain you, as long as you struggle to remain, in effect, suspended between two incompatible elements—one of butterflies, and one of mud. An early manuscript version of the passage excludes "the dream" element, and thus the ambiguity; see Kenneth Newell, "The Destructive Element and Related 'Dream' Passages in the *Lord Jim* Manuscript," *Journal of Modern Literature* 1 (1970): 31–44.

20. Robert Heilman first called Jim a "tragic hero," a view which was qualified and endorsed by Dorothy Van Ghent. See Heilman, Introduction, *Lord Jim* (New York: Rinehart, 1957); and Van Ghent, *The English Novel: Form and Function* (New York: Rinehart, 1953).

21. Ian Watt, "The Ending of *Lord Jim*," *Conradiana* 11 (1979): 100.

22. For a taxonomy of Marlow's deceptions, see Guerard (note 4), chapter 5. J. Hillis Miller sees Marlow's "doubt of the sovereign power enthroned in a fixed standard of conduct" as the central motivation for *Lord Jim*'s structure; see *Fiction and Repetition: Seven English Novels* (Cambridge: Harvard Univ. Press, 1982), 22–42. In *The Novel and the*

Modern World, David Daiches argues that Conrad doesn't really believe in the ideals of conduct he seems to promote (Chicago: Univ. of Chicago Press, 1960), 26–45. Daiches and Marlow both confuse failure to implement a code with either a fraudulent code or disingenuous belief in it.

23. Kenneth Bruffee, *Elegiac Romance: Cultural Change and Loss of the Hero in Modern Fiction* (Ithaca: Cornell Univ. Press, 1983), 110, 73.

24. Jameson (note 9) especially, "Magical Narratives," 103–50; and "Romance and Reification," 206–79.

25. Jameson, 114, 117.

26. Chinua Achebe makes Jameson's argument more pointedly, claiming that Conrad is, in short, "a bloody racist"; see "An Image of Africa," *Research in African Literatures* 9 (1978): 1–15. Patrick Brantlinger steers a middle course between Achebe's view and those who defend Conrad absolutely; see "Epilogue: Kurtz's 'Darkness' and Conrad's *Heart of Darkness*," in *Rule of Darkness: British Literature and Imperialism, 1830–1914* (Ithaca: Cornell Univ. Press, 1988), 255–74.

27. Reprinted in *Joseph Conrad on Fiction*, ed. Walter F. Wright (Lincoln: Univ. of Nebraska Press, 1964), 159–60.

28. Fleishman, "Reminiscing" (note 12), 22.

29. Mark Conroy takes Marlow's ambivalence to mirror Conrad's own, arguing that the novel's narrative strategies are intended to legitimate empire and reaffirm its values; see *Modernism and Authority: Strategies of Legitimation in Flaubert and Conrad* (Baltimore: Johns Hopkins Univ. Press, 1985), 99–117.

30. The book's second half prompted Leavis to dismiss the novel in "*Nostromo* and Minor Works," *The Great Tradition: A Study of the English Novel* (New York: Doubleday, 1954). Tanner (note 16) calls Patusan a "never-never land" which nevertheless completes the inquiries of the first half (47). For Tanner, though, the inquiry is whether Jim finally attains his dream, a much different question than the one I am posing here. Ian Watt (note 21) argues that the conventional literary modes of "fable, [or] fairy tale, and medieval romance" which convey the Patusan story create "a marked falling off from the moral and dramatic intensity" of the first part (10).

31. Suresh Raval also views Jim's idealism as inevitably destructive of the community's prospects for political stability; see *The Art of Failure: Conrad's Fiction* (Boston: Allen and Unwin, 1986).

32. Fleishman, *Conrad's Politics* (note 12), 57.

33. Fleishman, 69.

34. Bruffee (note 23), 131.

35. From the manuscript of the "Preface" in the Rosenbach Collection, cited in John Dozier Gordan, *Joseph Conrad: The Making of a Novelist* (Cambridge: Harvard Univ. Press, 1940).

36. Joseph Conrad, "The Inheritors," *New York Times*, 24 August 1901, 603, column 1.

37. My thanks go to Evan Carton, Jack Farrell, Charles Rossman and Mark Wollaeger for commenting on this essay's earlier drafts; and especially to Avrom Fleishman for his invaluable suggestions in its later stages.

Chronology

1856	May 8, Apollo Korzeniowski and Eva Bobrowska marry.
1857	December 3, Birth of Józef Teodor Konrad Walecz Korzeniowski.
1861	Family living in Warsaw. October: Apollo arrested and imprisoned for political activities.
1862	Family deported to Vologda.
1865	April 18, Eva dies.
1869	Apollo and Conrad move to Cracow. May 23, Death of Apollo. Conrad becomes ward of his uncle Tadeusz Bobrowski.
1872	Conrad states desire to go to sea.
1873	May: Conrad travels with tutor to Switzerland.
1874	Departs for Marseilles. First voyage, as passenger, on *Mont-Blanc*, and then sails as an apprentice.
1876	July 8, Sails the *Saint-Antoine* for the West Indies. Meets Dominic Cervoni.
1878	February: Attempts suicide. June: Departs for England. July: Sails on *Skimmer of the Seas* around British Isles.
1879	Sails on *Duke of Sutherland* to Australia and on *Europa* to Mediterranean.
1880	June: passes his exam for second mate. August: Departs on the *Loch Etive*, bound for Australia.

1881	September: Sails as second mate on steamship *Palestine* to the Indian Ocean.
1883	March: Cargo on *Palestine* catches fire and ship is abandoned. July: Conrad vacations with Tadeusz.
1884	April: Sails on the *Narcissus* to Bombay. December: passes first mate's exam.
1886	August: becomes a naturalized British citizen. Passes exam for master's certificate. Wrote first short story "The Black Mate".
1887	February: Joins sailing ship, *Highland Forest*, as first mate. Checks into hospital in Singapore. Signs on steamship *Vidar*. Meets the original Almayer.
1888	Sails on *Otago*, his only command as captain.
1889	Returns to England, begins writing first novel, *Almayer's Folly*. November: Interviews with shipping company in Brussels for a position in the Congo.
1890	Meets Marguerite Poradowska. Visits uncle in Poland. Appointed captain of river steam on the Congo. Arrives in the Congo in June.
1891	Returns from Congo, ill and exhausted. Goes for convalescence at Champel, near Geneva. November: Sails on the *Torrens*.
1892	Meets John Galsworthy and Edward Sanderson.
1893	Travels to Ukraine for his last visit with Tadeusz Bobrowski. Goes to Rouen to sail on the *Adowa*.
1894	*Adowa* trip canceled. February: Tadeusz Bobrowski dies. October: *Almayer's Folly* accepted at Fisher Unwin. Conrad meets Edward Garnett. November: Meets Jessie George.
1895	April: *Almayer's Folly* published.
1896	March 24: Marries Jessie George. Go to Brittany for honeymoon. *An Outcast of the Island* published. He begins working on *The Rescue*.
1897	Moves to Ivy walls. Meets Cunninghame Graham and Stephen Crane. *The Nigger of the "Narcissus"* published. Relationship with *Blackwood's Magazine* begins.

1898	*Tales of Unrest* published. First son, Borys, born. Meets Ford Madox Ford. Moves to Pent Farm. Collaboration with Ford.
1900	*Lord Jim* published. J.B Pinker becomes agent.
1901	*The Inheritors* (with Ford) published.
1902	*Youth* published.
1903	*Typhoon* volume and *Romance* (with Ford) published.
1904	Jessie falls, injures her knee. *Nostromo* published.
1905	Trip to Europe. Play *One Day More* performed.
1906	*The Mirror of the Sea* published. Second son, John, born. Trip to Europe.
1907	*The Secret Agent* published. Moves to Someries, Bedfordshire.
1908	*A Set of Six* published.
1909	Moves to Aldington, Kent.
1910	"The Secret Sharer" appears in *Harper's Magazine*. Quarrels with Ford, then Pinker. Has nervous breakdown. Moves to Capel House.
1911	*Under Western Eyes* published. Receives Civil List Pension.
1912	*'Twixt Land and Sea* and *A Personal Record* published. Meets Richard Curle.
1913	Success of *Chance* in America and England.
1914	Visit to Poland, World War I breaks out. With difficulty, the family makes their way back to England.
1915	Borys enlists. *Victory* published, highly successful. *Within the Tides* published.
1917	*The Shadow-Line* published.
1919	Moves to Oswalds. *The Arrow of Gold* published. Begins dramatization of *The Secret Agent*. Sells film rights to his works.
1920	*The Rescue* published. Begins working on *Suspense*, an unfinished novel.
1921	Trip to Corsica. *Notes on Life and Letters* published.
1923	Visits America. Borys marries. *The Rover* published.
1924	Sits for Jacob Epstein bust. Declines knighthood. July: has heart attack. August 3: Dies. Buried at Canterbury.

1925   *Tales of Hearsay and Suspense* posthumously published.
1926   *Last Essays* published.

Works by Joseph Conrad

Almayer's Folly, 1865.
An Outcast of the Islands, 1896.
The Nigger of the "Narcissus": A Tale of the Sea, 1897.
Tales of Unrest, 1898.
Lord Jim: A Tale, 1900.
The Inheritors, an Extravagant Story, co-author Ford, 1901.
Youth: A Narrative; and Two Other Stories, includes "Heart of Darkness,"
    serialized in 1899, 1902.
Typhoon and Other Stories, 1903.
Romance, co-author Ford, 1903.
Nostromo: A Tale of the Seaboard, 1904.
The Mirror of the Sea: Memories and Impressions, 1906.
The Secret Agent: A Simple Tale, 1907.
A Set of Six, 1908.
Under Western Eyes, 1911.
A Personal Record, 1912.
'Twixt Land and Sea: Tales, includes "The Secret Sharer," 1912.
Chance: A Tale In Two Parts, 1913.
Victory: An Island Tale, 1915.
With the Tides: Tales, 1915.
The Shadow-Line: A Confession, 1917.
The Arrow of Gold: A Story between Two Notes, 1919.
The Rescue: A Romance of the Shallows, 1920.
Notes on Life and Letters, 1921.

The Rover, 1923.
Suspense: A Napoleonic Novel, unfinished, 1925.
Tales of Hearsay, 1925.
Last Essays, 1926.
The Sisters, written in 1896, unfinished, 1928.

Works about Joseph Conrad

Baines, Jocelyn. *Joseph Conrad: A Critical Biography*. New York: McGraw-Hill, 1960.

Berman, Jeffrey. *Joseph Conrad: Writing as Rescue*. New York: Astra Books, 1977.

Bloom, Harold, editor. *Joseph Conrad*. New York: Chelsea House Publishers, 1986.

Conrad, Jessie, *Joseph Conrad and His Circle*. Port Washington, NY: Kennikat Press, 1964.

Fogel, Aaron. *Coercion to Speak: Conrad's Poetics of Dialogue*. Cambridge: Harvard University Press, 1985.

Ford, Ford Madox. *Joseph Conrad: A Personal Remembrance*. Boston: Little, Brown & Co., 1924.

Karl, Frederick. *Joseph Conrad: The Three Lives*. New York: Farrar, Straus & Giroux, 1979.

———. With Laurence Davies, editors. *The Collected Letters of Joseph Conrad, Volume 1, 1861-1897*. Cambridge: Cambridge University Press, 1983.

Garnett, Edward. *Letters from Joseph Conrad, 1895-1924*. Indianapolis: Bobbs-Merrill, 1928.

Gillon, Adam. *Joseph Conrad*. Boston: Twayne Publishers, 1982.

Guerard, Albert J. *Conrad the Novelist*. Cambridge: Harvard University Press, 1958.

———. *Joseph Conrad*. New York: New Directions, 1947.

Jean-Aubry, Gerard. *The Sea Dreamer: A Definitive Biography of Joseph Conrad*. New York: Archon Books, 1967.

Meyer, Bernard C. *Joseph Conrad: A Psychoanalytic Biography*. Princeton: Princeton University Press, 1967.

Meyers, Jeffrey. *Joseph Conrad: A Biography*. New York: Charles Scribner's Sons, 1991.

Najder, Zdzislaw. *Joseph Conrad: A Chronicle*. Trans. Halina Carroll-Najder. New Brunswick, NJ: Rutgers University Press, 1983.

Sherry, Norman. *Conrad*. New York: Thames & Hudson, 1972.

Tennant, Roger. *Joseph Conrad: A Biography*. New York: Atheneum Publishers, 1981.

Watt, Ian. *Conrad in the Nineteenth Century*. Berkeley: University of California Press, 1979.

WEBSITES

Joseph Conrad Foundation
members.tripod.com/~JTKNK/

The Joseph Conrad Society
www.bathspa.ac.uk/conrad/

Joseph Conrad Pages
www.stfrancis.edu/en/student/kurtzweb/conrad.htm

Joseph Conrad—The Victorian Web
65.107.211.206/authors/conrad/conradov.html

Author Profile for Joseph Conrad (BBC)
www.bbc.co.uk/arts/books/author/conrad/

Contributors

HAROLD BLOOM is Sterling Professor of the Humanities at Yale University and Henry W. and Albert A. Berg Professor of English at the New York University Graduate School. He is the author of over 20 books, including *Shelley's Mythmaking* (1959), *The Visionary Company* (1961), *Blake's Apocalypse* (1963), *Yeats* (1970), *A Map of Misreading* (1975), *Kabbalah and Criticism* (1975), *Agon: Toward a Theory of Revisionism* (1982), *The American Religion* (1992), *The Western Canon* (1994), and *Omens of Millennium: The Gnosis of Angels, Dreams, and Resurrection* (1996). *The Anxiety of Influence* (1973) sets forth Professor Bloom's provocative theory of the literary relationships between the great writers and their predecessors. His most recent books include *Shakespeare: The Invention of the Human* (1998), a 1998 National Book Award finalist, *How to Read and Why* (2000), and *Genius: A Mosaic of One Hundred Exemplary Creative Minds* (2002). In 1999, Professor Bloom received the prestigious American Academy of Arts and Letters Gold Medal for Criticism, and in 2002 he received the Catalonia International Prize.

AMY SICKLES is a freelance writer living in New York City. She has published short stories, essays, and book reviews in numerous journals, including *Fourth Genre*, *Kalliope*, and *Literary Review*. She has taught at Pennsylvania State University and holds a B.A. from Ohio University and a Master of Fine Arts in Creative Writing from Pennsylvania State University.

RICHARD RUPPEL is the Chair of the English at Viterbo University. He is the coeditor with Philip Holden of *Imperial Desires: Dissident Sexualities and Colonial Literature*, 2003. He has also published numerous articles on Joseph Conrad.

CAROLA M. KAPLAN is Professor of English and Foreign Languages at California State Polytechnic University, Pomona. She is the coeditor with Anne B. Simpson of Seeing *Double: Revisioning Edwardian and Modernist Literature*, 1996. In addition to numerous articles on Conrad, she has also written on E.M. Forster, Graham Greene, and Flannery O'Connor.

DAVID ALLEN WARD is a Lecturer in Professional Communication at the University of Wisconsin-Madison. He has also published essays on Jane Austen, Charles Dickens, and Matthew Arnold.

TRACY SEELEY is an Associate Professor in the English Department at the University of San Francisco, specializing in Modernist, Victorian, and Postcolonial Literature. She has published on Joseph Conrad, Virginia Woolf, and Victorian women essayists.

INDEX